THE
REVOLUTION
DISARMED

To the workers of my country
whose blood will not have
been shed in vain on the day
when imperialism and the
bourgeoisie are defeated.

THE REVOLUTION DISARMED

CHILE 1970-1973

GABRIEL SMIRNOW

Monthly Review Press
New York and London

Library of Congress Cataloging in Publication Data
Smirnow, Gabriel
    The revolution disarmed, Chile, 1970-1973.
    Translation of La revolución desarmada, Chile, 1970-1973.
    Includes bibliographical references.
    1. Socialism in Chile.   2. Chile—Politics and government—1970-
3. Chile—Economic conditions—1970-   4. Chile—Social conditions
—1970-   I. Title.
HX198.5.S6313   335'.00983   79-83500
ISBN 0-85345-443-4
ISBN 0-85345-486-8 pbk.

Monthly Review Press
62 West 14th Street, New York, N.Y. 10011
47 Red Lion Street, London WC1R 4PF

Manufactured in the United States of America

10 9 8 7 6 5 4 3 2 1

CONTENTS

Introduction   1

1 April 1971: Advances and Retreats   9

2 The Debate over the Middle Classes   18

3 The Economic Program and Laws of the Market   33

4 Development of the Class Struggle   48

5 October 1972: The First Bourgeois Insurrection   65

6 Popular Power   81

7 March 1973:
   The "Parliamentary Road" of the Right   100

8 The Institutions of the Capitalist State   119

9 September 1973: The Triumph of Reaction   140

10 A Chilean Road to Socialism?   157

INTRODUCTION

The various forms assumed by the capitalist system in Latin American societies substantially reflect the traditional mechanisms of domination that have been developed by each country's ruling classes.

At a time in Chile when democracy was deepening its roots, when the level of organization and consciousness among the workers was rising and rifts were appearing in the broad spectrum of bourgeois interests, the wielders of economic, social, and political power acted true to their own tradition in yielding the presidency to Salvador Allende and the Popular Unity (Unidad Popular) coalition on November 4, 1970. Thus began a process whose originality drew attention and study not only among opponents of the capitalist system but among its defenders.

For the first time in Latin American and world history, a self-declared Marxist and an alliance of parties based on communist-socialist unity took over by democratic elections the administration of state affairs in a capitalist and dependent country.

The subsequent barefaced intervention of multinational enterprises and U.S. government agencies against the Popular Unity administration; the democratic and pluralist character of that administration and the advance of revolutionary forces during its mandate; the treason of plotting generals, and the fascistic violence which struck down the Chilean people—all these help to explain and justify the interest in this process and the tremendous solidarity evoked by the resistance to the dictatorship.

Yet the explanations offered for the defeat of the process that

1

unfolded during President Allende's one thousand days in government rarely go beyond the role of U.S. imperialist intervention and the criminality of the military mutineers against the constitutional regime. The presence of CIA agents on Chilean soil since before Allende's accession is now a matter of public knowledge and beyond dispute. Likewise known are the CIA's financing of the reactionary newspaper *El Mercurio* and other media, its participation in the murder of constitutionalist Gen. René Schneider, its aid in subsidizing thousands of truck owners who twice acted as detonators of seditious bourgeois movements. Even more important was the "economic blockade" which Allende several times denounced (for instance, at the United Nations on December 4, 1972), involving cancellation of loans and credits by all U.S.-controlled financial agencies and private concerns, suspension of imports, stiffer conditions for servicing the external debt, an embargo on copper shipments—in sum, an agglomeration of "legal" activities that brought semichaos to the economy of a country as traditionally dependent on the United States as Chile was in November 1970.

The Chilean experience was a serious threat to imperialist interests for strategic reasons reaching far beyond that country's borders, and thus evoked the concentrated attention and effort of the U.S. government departments concerned. As early as September 14, 1970, before the president-elect took office, the "possibility" that he would do so was discussed by Secretary of State Kissinger in the following terms:

> It is fairly easy to predict that if Allende wins, there are many possibilities for the establishment of a sort of Communist government over a period of years. In that case we would not have a government of this type on an island lacking traditional relations with or impact on Latin America, but a Communist government sharing, for example, a long frontier with Argentina—a country already deeply divided—and contiguous with Peru, which has been moving in directions that make dealings with it difficult, and with Bolivia, which has also been moving in a more or less Left direction, against the United States, which has none of these characteristics. So I don't think we should delude ourselves that Allende's rise to power in Chile does not present massive problems for us, for the democratic forces in Latin America favorable to us, and certainly for the whole Western Hemisphere.

The treason of the generals led by Augusto Pinochet is also well enough known. On a strictly ethical basis, the man betrayed that "word of honor" so prized in military circles. But he did this with the whole of the armed forces behind him, and performed in the same way as all of Chile's state institutions, which, while owing respect and allegiance to the Constitution, formed an integral part of the plot to defeat the workers and put an end to democracy.

U.S. imperialism acts so obviously in defense of its own interests that any popular leader proposing to act against those interests must be prepared for a confrontation. Similarly, the role of the armed forces, in Latin America particularly and in the capitalist world generally, is part of a political culture well known to Chilean leaders (including all the national military institutions).

Consequently, any simplistic explanation of President Allende's overthrow tends to camouflage, or attempts to ignore or minimize, the tactical mistakes and intrinsic errors of the Popular Unity government's three-year program.

Unlike most of the rest of Latin America, in Chile the labor movement and the diffusion of socialist thought have a history going back to the end of the last century. The first big strikes were savagely suppressed, especially in the nitrate-mining zone characterized by foreign exploitation and the concentration of thousands of workers in small urban centers. Thus in 1907, 1921, and 1925 the army crushed the workers' economic and social demands with full-dress massacres, resulting in the retreat of the nascent proletariat's organizations. But these organizations continued to grow and, after Luis Emilio Recabarren founded the Socialist Workers Party in 1912, maintained the independent class character necessary to pursue their own political goals. In 1938 began a period of modernization of economic structures led by the Radical Party, which became the voice of the new bourgeois, industrial, and commercial sectors and for many years displaced the Chilean oligarchy from the direct exercise of public power. For the workers this was a period of a diminished level of consciousness and organization and declining independent activity, since their movement became a tail to the reformist government's Popular Front program. In 1953 a new period of advance began, marked by massacres, legal struggles, and violently suppressed strikes, by the unionization of workers and campesinos (peasants), and by the growth of the parties of the Left, which found an even broader audience. Nineteen sixty-seven saw a new and decisive surge forward, beginning with the general strike called by the United Confederation of Workers (Central Unica de Trabajadores, CUT)—a demonstration of the power that workers led by the industrial proletariat had achieved in Chilean society. This new rise in popular struggle led to the victory of September 4, 1970—proof of the workers' capacity and potential to transform a social system that had never solved most of the population's basic problems nor even found a way to boost the economy in terms of satisfactory capitalist expansion.

By February 1971 delegates to the Socialist Party Congress were stressing that "the popular government is a tool for the workers' conquest of power"; but as later events showed, the tools could be well or badly used.

The Chilean process has given rise to a rare unanimity. Both the champions of the deep-going changes—whether by the "politico-institutional" or "revolutionary" road—and the opponents of such changes, such as the advocates of a "communitarian" or "authoritarian" state, agree that September 4, 1970, ushered in a period that threatened the stability of Chile's political institutions and hence all of its social and economic relations. In all social processes, and especially revolutionary ones, there is constant interaction between the opposing forces; one sector's errors spur the energies and firmness of the antagonist, tactical weaknesses end up as strategic weakness, and a theoretically fallacious program leads inevitably to its defeat in practice.

Hence, in tracing the different stages or influences in this process, one must point out that the actions of imperialism and the treachery of the generals are undoubtedly important but not fundamental. For these alone could not defeat a correlation of forces favorable to the workers, as historical experience in general and the Chilean in particular show.

The September 1970 elections were held in a tripolar situation, with Jorge Alessandri as the National Party's and Radical Democrats' candidate, Radomiro Tomic as the Christian Democrats', and Salvador Allende as the candidate of Popular Unity. A brief explanation of how the nonsocialist forces came to be divided is required, for this also contains important keys to understanding how the confrontation within state institutions developed.

In the 1964 presidential elections a disquieting phenomenon had already emerged for the political parties offering Chilean society and its economy different models of capitalist administration, from the standpoint of different ruling-class sectors. There were initially three candidates: Julio Durán for the Radical, Liberal, and Conservative parties, Eduardo Frei for the Christian Democrats, and Allende for the organizations that would later form Popular Unity. An unexpected election to replace a deputy showed evidence of an impressive advance by the Left. It was clear by any analysis that if all three presidential candidates ran, Allende would win a first-round majority. So the Conservatives and Liberals hurriedly removed support from the candidate best representing their interests and united their electoral efforts behind Frei, who won with more than half the votes.

As president, Frei introduced a program of modernizing Chile's backward economic structures, especially the agrarian. Under a reform of some importance, part of the land passed into the hands of a sector which thereby raised its consumption levels and stimulated industrial production. But at the same time, that policy antagonized the Chilean oligarchy with its major interests in the countryside. Frei's economy-boosting program was linked to more dynamic elements of the industrial bourgeoisie who, especially in the utilization of state-distributed credits, forcibly displaced the monopolies traditionally holding the reins of power. This opened a deep rift between Christian Democracy and the newly created National Party (which was created through a merger of the Conservative and Liberal parties).

Beginning in 1967, the country's economy entered a period of severe stagnation. The average growth-rate for the four years 1967-1970 was 2.7 percent a year, barely more than the population growth (2.3 percent) and certainly below the growth rate of almost all Latin American countries. In the same period, by official figures, unemployment rose to an average 5.2 percent of the active population (National Planning Office, 1971).

Further proof of the failure of Frei's attempts at reform, which clashed with inexorable laws of capitalist accumulation and concentration, is the fact that in 1970, 1,265,000 workers received less than the *sueldos vitales.** This sector as a whole, representing nearly 50 percent of the active population, received 12 percent of the national income.

---

*During President Ibáñez' administration this was a family subsistence wage. It later lost this meaning, and the term was used in a statistical context. By the end of the Frei administration, the "minimum wage" was more than two *sueldos vitales,* and their purchasing power was less than one initial *sueldo vital.*

The Chilean economy had definitely entered a period of net stagnation which only revolutionary or intensely reformist policies could break. In either case this had to affect—in different degrees—the most backward bourgeois sectors which directly profited by the situation. Allende stood for a program of profound change while the Christian Democrats took the road of developmentalist reform led by the "progressive" sector under Tomic.

Thus a repetition of the party alliance that gave Frei the victory in 1964 was prevented by historical causes and by necessarily different economic programs. In 1970 the "economic Right," identified with the "political Right," raised its electoral sails under the captaincy of septuagenarian Alessandri, who won many more votes than Christian Democrat reformist Tomic but was defeated by Allende with a trifling majority.

On the night of September 4 the mansions of the Chilean propertied class were taken by surprise: with 36.3 percent of the votes, Allende had won a plurality (Alessandri 34.9 percent, Tomic 27.8) and according to institutional tradition would assume the presidency.

During the sixty days between the elections and the assumption of power, the popular movement remained on the defensive with all its forces tensed in expectation. But what essentially characterized this period was the ruling-class split into two programs—a split that would continue for a certain time. One sector proposed to limit and reduce the Popular Unity program by binding it to constitutional tradition; with the popular forces' goals thus curtailed, its content would be reduced to mere reformism. The other, more aware of the social forces that had been unleashed, proposed to prevent implementation of the program from the outset, even at the price of smashing the tradition to which almost all Chilean party leaders pointed with pride.

From the first days after the elections it was plain that those rules of the game, so laboriously laid down over the forty preceding years, had quickly lost their usefulness for maintaining bourgeois domination: they had become expendable. Since legality—"their legality"—no longer served, the ruling classes did not hesitate to court danger by seeking to subvert public order. So began the flight of capital, the purpose of which was to create panic among the petty and middle propertied bourgeoisie and to topple the country's economy—a maneuver aided by Christian Democratic minister Andrés Zaldívar and the CIA. In *Subver-*

sion in Chile: A Case Study in U.S. Corporate Intrigue in the Third World, which was published in Chile by the state publishing house Quimantú, we find the report submitted by agent Robert Berrellez on September 29: "Despite the pessimism, efforts are continuing to move Frei and/or the military to act to stop Allende." Further, "undercover efforts are being made to bring about the bankruptcy of one or two major savings and loan associations. This is expected to trigger a run on banks and the closure of some factories resulting in more unemployment."

When this failed, commander-in-chief of the army René Schneider was assassinated in the latter part of October 1970 for refusing to collaborate in a coup d'état with the commander of the Santiago army garrison, the commander-in-chief of the navy, and the Director General of Carabineros (police)—a plot organized by retired Gen. Roberto Viaux with the participation of a sector of the Christian Democrats. Viaux's statement in the book *Conversaciones con Viaux* (Conversations with Viaux) has never been denied: "Finally, around the third week in September, I learned from my contacts that Señor Frei would dare to act. I also learned that Treasury Minister Señor Zaldivar would issue a report—as in fact he did—characterizing the country's economic-financial situation as unfavorable." He goes on: "It must have been around the first week in October that don Guillermo Carey told me the president [Frei] now wanted a coup which would bring in a military junta and exile the president, on condition that Señor Frei's part in all this would not be known." In other words, Frei was guarding his democratic image at any cost, to retain the possibility of winning back the presidency later on.

However, the would-be rebels failed to enlist the whole of the armed forces and hence could not carry out their conspiracy. An important fraction of Christian Democracy was simultaneously negotiating with Allende the so-called Statute of Guarantees as a constitutional amendment, in exchange for their votes in the Congressional Plenum* without which he could not be confirmed as president of the Republic. The essence of these statutes was a limitation on the executive's authority and initiative, making it more dependent on the Congress, especially with respect to various points in the Popular Unity program.

* Meeting of the two chambers of Congress.

In this way the "progressive" Christian Democratic sector showed its claws, all the while affirming its respect for Chilean constitutional tradition. Confident that this was enough to hold the popular forces within the boundaries of the Constitution approved by the bourgeoisie in 1925, it accepted a program of important reforms as long as these were adjusted to the line and ideology maintained and affirmed by the ruling class.

Astounded but far from impotent, U.S. imperialism and a large part of the Chilean bourgeoisie saw the first admitted Marxist, "freely and democratically" elected, invested as president on November 4, 1970.

As we have said, the ruling class without an instant's hesitation began resorting to every possible method of confronting the threat to its interests, represented by Popular Unity. In this it did no more than confirm basic principles of Marxist theory and of universal historical experience: a live organism facing death resists its enemy with all the means at its disposal. And the Chilean propertied class enjoyed excellent health. After failing to bring about economic collapse and a coup d'état on the eve of the new administration's inauguration, the bourgeoisie withdrew in good order: weakened, divided, but without panic, weighing from that moment on the various alternatives of confrontation with the process that Allende's victory set in motion.

Popular Unity began its administration with a policy perspective that would not essentially change throughout the process: gradual transformation of the country's structures, avoidance of violent confrontation. More precisely, a program basically piloted by the Chilean Communist Party, which could be a direct and most valuable precedent for Communist Party policy developments in Italy and France.

As we examine the Popular Unity government's one thousand days, we will see how most leaders of the Left were incapable to the end of modifying the close adherence to "legality" which had given them partial power, and the nonviolent-institutional character which they sought to impose on the political process and class struggle in Chile.

Thus emerged an original and contradictory phenomenon: attempts to impose by peaceful means changes that were essentially revolutionary, against the ever fiercer resistance of the workers' enemies. The result is known; the responsibility rests on those who refused to take advantage of all the favorable conjunctures that arose to strike at the bourgeoisie and its institutions. This we propose to prove.

1 APRIL 1971:
ADVANCES AND RETREATS

Popular Unity's program was the fruit of intense discussion among the parties of the coalition. Communists, Socialists, Radicals, Social Democrats, API (Independent Popular Action), and MAPU (Movement for Unified Popular Action) represented different popular sectors, had different origins and traditions, and projected different economic, social, and political programs for the development of Chile.

Communists and Socialists constituted the core of a coalition in which the working class was quantitatively decisive. Both of those parties had a wide following among campesinos, white-collar workers, *pobladores,** students, artisans, and small merchants. The Radicals, Social Democrats, and API represented a broad cross-section of the middle stratum, including small industrialists, businessmen, profes-

---

*The struggle of the "homeless" *(sin casa)* arose with the phenomenon of rapid urbanization. This struggle can be characterized as follows: to begin with a group of homeless families organized themselves (often with the aid of a left-wing political organization), and without notice occupied a parcel of unused land, which might be privately or state-owned. They would erect shacks of pieces of wood and tin and raise the Chilean flag. This was a *toma*, a land take-over. Later, if they were not evicted, the inhabitants would make improvements in their wretched shanties and would attempt to lay out streets; new residents would arrive and the "takeover" would acquire a certain legitimacy, transforming itself into a *campamento*. Later the *campamento* would receive electric power, some of the

sionals, and public officials, but carried less weight: they were a clear minority, not only numerically but also in what they could contribute to the transformations that were deemed necessary.

It fell to the Socialist Party to put forward Allende's candidacy as the voice of the workers' parties in the role they had to play. This was "to begin the construction of socialism," as the Popular Unity program put it in a resolution passed only after a severe struggle against certain tendencies, particularly sectors with roots in the institutional history of Chile as administrators.

The discussions within the Popular Unity on the candidate, which also included discussions on the orientation of the program, had gone on for several months, especially between the Radical and Communist parties on the one hand, and the Socialist Party on the other. The former wanted a program that would be more "moderate" than the final version that was ultimately adopted; in fact, they even rejected the candidacy of Salvador Allende who, they claimed, presented a negative image because of his defeat in prior presidential elections. It was the firmness of the Socialist Party and its threat to withdraw from the coalition and present its own candidate that in the end forced the Radicals and Communists to accept Allende's candidacy.

As a result, however, the Popular Unity program was markedly flavored with ambiguity and compromise. Yet it correctly characterized Chilean society as capitalist and dependent, and the measures it put forward pointed toward a deep transformation of social and economic relations. On the level of anti-imperialist goals it proposed to nationalize the chief mining enterprises—copper, iron, nitrates, coal—most of which were in U.S. hands, as well as to statify a considerable number of large industrial monopolies and the banking system which belonged to multinational concerns and the big financial bourgeoisie of Chile. The agricultural program called for total disappearance of the latifundia

---

streets would be paved, the houses began to be constructed of brick, and the residents acquired a definitive legal status. It is then a *población*. Of course this entire process can take months or even years, depending on circumstances, and the dividing lines between *campamento* and *población* are often blurred. The inhabitants themselves can contribute to the confusion, which is one not only of language but also of status, etc.

through expropriation of all estates exceeding the equivalent of eighty irrigated hectares, and for new forms of cooperative and state farms. Industrially, the program called for expropriation of the ninety-one chief manufacturing units, the most dynamic and important part of Chilean industry, thus providing the basis for a Social Production Sector. Workers' participation in management of state enterprises introduced a new and revolutionary note into traditional production relations. In the electoral-legislative system suffrage was to be extended to new strata of the population and a single legislative chamber was projected. The judiciary was to be profoundly changed by a new system of electing judges and by the creation of people's courts. All these measures were calculated to crack open the traditional system of capitalist domination, open the road to its destruction, and set in motion the building of socialism, as the outgrowth of a new relation of class forces.

There was, however, considerable ambiguity in this program of revolutionary changes. It envisaged the machinery to change the relation of forces in the workers' favor but did not spell out just how the bourgeoisie would be made to disappear as a class. On the contrary, it offered guarantees for that class's preservation, trusting that the resolution of the problem could be postponed to the indeterminate future. In other words, the problem of power was posed only in a mechanical way, based on Chile's democratic and institutional development in the previous forty years and on the new relationships that were developing internationally. Thus the Popular Unity program projected a class alliance led by the proletariat which would embrace a wide range of interests, including the nonmonopolist bourgeoisie, under the generic name of "middle classes." At the same time it sought to pass over the social and political role historically played by the Chilean armed forces, as a polity separated from society and especially alien to working-class goals and demands.

We may say in synthesis that this program of profound change projected a "politico-institutional" nonviolent transformation, mainly of economic and social structures which would be gradually modified, wearing down the resistance—likewise within established democratic laws which could, however, be considerably broadened—to be expected from imperialism and the bourgeoisie. The changes would permit new class relations of forces to be generated, so that the transformation of political structures would be effected stage by stage and "at the lowest possible social cost." From the outset the Popular Unity government attempted to derive most of its power from the legality that put it in office. We will soon see how this legality became the main source of weakness for the whole revolutionary process and, at a given moment, hobbled the constitutional regime and undermined its authority.

By April 1971, Popular Unity, identified with the government, had enormously increased its popularity. Income was being radically redistributed, unemployment and inflation were manifestly lower, and expropriations, nationalizations and agrarian reform had been initiated. Meanwhile, the bourgeoisie was still split—as evidenced by the Christian Democrats' and Nationalists' continuing differences of political position. Still more important was the tireless activity of the masses, the first signs of which were becoming evident on all levels. Socialist and Communist party membership grew daily and solid foundations remained for agreement between the two parties on immediate measures. Trade unions expanded in city and countryside and a political awakening spread across the land.

It was in these favorable circumstances that municipal elections took place, in which 51 percent of the votes went to Left parties, with Christian Democrats and Nationalists dividing the rest. And in that situation the Socialist Party proposed a plebiscite aimed at replacing the two-chambered National Congress, which was now becoming the chief bastion of confrontation with the Left's program, by a unicameral body elected more democratically. Such a plebiscite was provided for in the Constitution during the Frei period and the opposition forces would demand it on various occasions in 1973 when electoral conditions became more auspicious for them.

In this way the Socialist Party sought, within the "institutional respect" extolled by Allende, to speed up the process which the election results showed to be fully feasible. As Socialist Party general secretary Carlos Altamirano would remind Communist general secretary Luis Corvalán in an open letter, it was the Communists who applied the brake: "In this respect we Socialists, aware that any apparent or real weakness on our part encourages the adversary and disheartens the working masses, have always opposed the conciliatory attitudes toward the class enemy, such as the rejection of our party's proposal immediately after the April 1971 municipal elections to call a plebiscite which would have capitalized on the electoral victory then won by Popular Unity. . . ."[1]

This was indeed an extraordinary opportunity—perhaps the greatest within the politico-institutional framework—to advance without excessive risk to the government's stability. The proof is the fact that the division of the bourgeoisie into two contradictory models of opposition made it impossible for them to confront a Popular Unity challenge with the necessary energy. At that time the ruling classes had yet to recover from the September defeat, and the April elections further disoriented them. Furthermore, important Christian Democratic sectors actively or passively supported the anti-imperialist measures, which at the same time forced some National Party sectors into prudent silence. (Later Congress would vote unanimously for the law nationalizing the big U.S.-owned copper mines.)

Also to be stressed is that in this situation the military groups favoring a coup d'état remained very weak, as a consequence of the abortive coup in October 1970. So that three conditions existed in April 1971 which would not recur: most of the electorate was behind Popular Unity, the bourgeois opposition had failed to reunify since their two alternative models remained on the agenda in mutual contradiction, and most of the repressive apparatus remained overwhelmingly loyal to the constitutional regime.

Certainly it is hard to say what would have happened had the Socialist proposal been accepted, but there is no doubt that the conditions for clinching the government's and popular movement's initiatives would have improved. A successful plebiscite would certainly have reduced the capacity of the bourgeoisie's representatives in Congress to maneuver and obstruct.

The Communist Party's negative reply was no accident. As early as November 1970 it had gained the majority position in Popular Unity leadership through its line of reaching an understanding with Christian Democracy.[2] This policy of dialogue with the chief opponents of Allende's government conformed to its class-alliance and economic development strategy; and that strategy would never be abandoned throughout the whole period, despite the different line advocated by important sectors—sometimes forming a majority—of Popular Unity's other principal component, the Socialist Party.

In effect, even before April 1971 two different tactics or strategies began to show up inside the Left parties; both supported the government program, each party put a different interpretation on it. We will see these tendencies taking on definition in course of the process, but already in May 1971 the left wing of the Socialist Party stated its position in such forceful terms as these:

The winning of the government, and above all of the presidency now in a Socialist's hands, gives the popular movement an unprecedented instrument with which to speed destruction of the bourgeois order and begin building a socialist society. Chilean workers see this victory as the result of a long history marked by massacres and martyrs. The proletariat has persisted in this struggle in order to establish socialism, not to stop halfway down the road. We must not of course forget that a process has to follow a certain rhythm in accordance with the forces participating in it, and that capitalist bastions must be destroyed step by step. But all the more is it absolutely necessary to maintain our objective—socialism—as a short-run objective. The April 4 elections have shown that the majority of Chile's people and workers want to pursue with audacity the march toward a new society. If elections within the bourgeois juridical framework have any value, it is precisely to measure the degree of consciousness achieved by the proletariat. Today we stand at a decisive moment in Chilean proletarian consciousness, with a mandate to press forward now with certain key objectives which have become immediate tasks:

1. Destruction of imperialism's economic and institutional base in our country and limitation of the national bourgeoisie's power. In line with this it is also necessary to speed up nationalizations and unmask Christian Democracy once and for all.

2. Democratization of the legislature and judiciary—objectives that are closely linked since, following the elections, the defiance of popular will by these two organs of the bourgeoisie becomes quite unacceptable. It is now the *immediate* responsibility of President Allende's government to dissolve these two powers.

3. Democratization of the military. A concrete plan is needed for active involvement of the armed forces as a conscious element in the current of majority will. This is not solely a government task. On the contrary, Socialists should stimulate discussion of the issue and make the whole popular movement aware of it.

Armed confrontation between the classes is inevitable. We believe that the strategic and tactical concepts expressed in resolutions of the Chillán (1967) and La Serena (1971) congresses remain valid with respect not only to the development of a Workers' Front as a strategy of class regroupment, but also to the affirmation that the effective conquest of power, destruction of the bourgeois state apparatus, and socialization of the means of production must inevitably pass through an armed confrontation between the classes to suppress reactionary and bourgeois sedition.

Reaction will again knock at the barracks doors and we must remember that the armed forces—with all the qualities we recognize, their traditional respect for the Constitution and government—have in the past been obliged to take an active part in repression. We have confidence in the patriotic sentiments and love of liberty that undoubtedly inspire the men serving under our flag, but Lenin's words are pertinent to our situation: "It seems impossible to fight against a modern army, the army has to become revolutionary. . . . In reality the indecision of the troops, inevitable in any truly popular movement, leads to a real struggle for the army as the revolutionary struggle intensifies."

In consequence, not to mince words, we must first win over the masses; and this is not a matter of vague sympathy or a good election result, but of mobilizing the combativeness of the working class in their unions and in their communities outside the CUT framework.

A process is under way and it cannot be stopped short of socialism. Therefore we must be the vanguard and prepare ourselves to rise to the height of this historic opportunity.[3]

At that time the outlines of the Chilean Left's two main tendencies were coming into focus. Those who would later be known as the revolutionary Left had matured considerably in their tactical and strategic ideas. At the outset the Movement of the Revolutionary Left (MIR) had sat out the elections that gave Allende the presidency, on the basis of a simplistic analysis of historical experience and Marxist-Leninist thought. Likewise, important sectors of the Socialist Party had shown little enthusiasm during the campaign. For these tendencies, struggles within the bourgeois-democratic electoral system were futile. Unconvinced that the presidency could be won by this route, they minimized the possibility of deepening democratic victories that stemmed from Chilean social traditions as well as from decades of organizing, consciousness-raising, and confrontation by the workers. Life turned out to be richer than experience. However, the revolutionary Left matured fast with respect to the process begun on September 4 and the possibilities it opened for the popular movement. The article we have quoted also marks an advance in the understanding of bourgeois state institutions, sounding a correct alarm as to the role of the armed forces.

The "politico-institutional road" program reflected a much better defined theoretical formulation of tactics, and dealt in detail with the possibilities of development and maneuver on the part of the government. Various factors now more shrewdly analyzed would allow a class alliance that would permit deep economic and social transformations: the separation of state powers, the decisive role of the Executive in Chile's economy with the statified sector as a base, the armed forces' neutrality toward struggles in the political superstructure since the early 1930s, the divisions among bourgeois sectors, and the split that had taken place at the level of political representation.

Joan Garcés, a close adviser to President Allende, thus summed up the possibilities: "In synthesis, the tactical measures that enabled the popular government to implement its policies in 1971 without causing a parliamentary crisis are (a) use of the broad freedom of action legally available to the administrative powers of the executive; (b) the studied effort to avoid conflict with the middle classes and their representative economic, social, and political institutions; (c) the government's decision to act within the institutional framework."[4]

As we proceed to analyze the consecutive stages and different aspects of the Chilean process we will show the deep-rooted strategic weakness that lay within this tactical opportunity. For despite all of Allende's and the Communist Party's efforts, the government and Popular Unity could not maintain the alliance with the "middle classes," nor persuade the rightist opposition that they were acting with strict respect for accepted institutions.

For the moment we only point out that a call for a plebiscite immediately following the April 1971 elections, looking toward a new and more important popular victory that would speed up the process, would have been in no way incompatible with the tactic outlined by the dominant sectors of Popular Unity and applied by the government. On the contrary, it was precisely at that moment—in a conjuncture of circumstances never to recur—that a rare possibility was offered to broaden the government's and the popular movement's margins of action within established constitutionality and legality, limiting and constricting the mechanisms of parliamentary opposition which the National Party was already beginning to use and which would end by uniting the whole bourgeoisie in an escalation of sedition.

1. Carlos Altamirano, *Decisión Revolucionaria* (Santiago de Chile: Quimantú, 1973).
2. Joan E. Garcés, *El Estado y los Problemas Tácticos en el Gobierno de Allende* (México: Siglo XXI, 1974).
3. Editorial, *Indoamérica* magazine (Santiago de Chile), No. 5, March 1971.
4. Garcés, *El Estado y los Problemas.*

2 THE DEBATE OVER
THE MIDDLE CLASSES

Having been chosen within a bourgeois-democratic institutional framework as a coalition of parties representing different strata and classes,
Popular Unity's class-alliance policy, which was the policy of the
Communist Party in particular, called for maintaining harmony among
diverse interests, especially on the social level. The intention was to
broaden the electoral support expressed in the election of April 1971.
At the same time, the low percentage of votes (slightly over 8 percent)
for the Radical Party, representing Popular Unity's petty- and middle-
bourgeois elements, forced the partisans of the "institutional road" into
greater efforts toward an understanding with Christian Democracy,
repugnant as this was to the Socialist Party.

Until then (mid-1971), although strategies differed, the forces comprising the government had a certain unanimity on implementation of
the projected transformations. At the stage the discussion focused on
the rhythm of the process rather than on basic differences. But from
this point on two facts emerged more and more plainly: the difficulty
of getting a consensus among divergent—if not contradictory and
antagonistic—interests, and the stable support on which Christian
Democracy could count in wide social sectors.

Thus the differences between Popular Unity's two main tendencies
intensified, and the polemic centered around the class-alliance policy
itself: the great debate over the role of the "middle classes" which
never ceased until the day of the military coup.

The various classes' roles had been analyzed and discussed from the
early days of the socialist movement. While ever since Marx's time the

different tendencies accepted the role of the proletariat as the main propellant, to this day they still differ about the alliances it should make to win victory for the revolutionary process. A problem of social and semantic definition helps obscure this discussion: Who are the "middle classes"?

In the Middle Ages society was based on autarchic units of production with two essential components: the nobility, and the serfs who worked the lands and performed other secondary labor. But from the thirteenth century, with the development first of commerce and then of manufacturing, new social classes appeared. By the eighteenth century the cities had large populations who, aside from belonging to neither of the above classes, were moved by different interests with strong mutual contradictions. By the mid-nineteenth century the differences became clear between the industrial, commercial, and financial bourgeoisie, the latter having entered the administration of public affairs in Europe after the French Revolution. However, the nobility retained a good share of political and economic power as well as social privileges, and thus was still classified as the "upper class." Between it and the so-called "lower classes" of workers and peasants, there was now a high percentage of the population moved by markedly different interests: the "middle classes."

Today, from both the sociological and the political point of view, the generic term "middle classes" is an unacceptable generalization, lending itself not only to confusion but to falsification of the social position of the most numerous sectors of the misnamed "middle classes." Indeed, to plan a policy of alliances, one must define the roles of the various social strata in production and exchange, their income levels, their professional standings, and the particular nature of their goals in order to determine their respective interests, which not only differ from sector to sector but are often in direct contradiction. The following charts of Chile's active population, published in *Nueva Economía*, journal of the National Planning Office (ODEPLAN), September-December 1971, are helpful:

Table 1
Distribution of Active Labor Force in 1970

	Thousands of persons	Percentages
Active population	3,189.2	100.00
Agriculture	738.0	23.14
Mining	99.2	3.11
Industry	567.3	17.79
Construction	177.5	5.56
Trade	451.5	14.15
Services	965.1	30.29
Unemployed	190.6	5.96

Table 2
Occupational Categories of Labor Force

	Thousands of persons	Percentages
Active employed population	2,998.6	100.00
Employers	48.0	1.6
Self-employed	665.7	22.2
White-collar workers	722.7	24.1
Blue-collar workers	1,388.3	46.3
Family members and others	173.9	5.8

It is not our present task to attempt new definitions for the various sectors of the heterogeneous bloc between proletariat and bourgeoisie. Artisans, professionals, small merchants, private white-collar employees, public officials, small and middle industrialists, small peasant proprietors—all make up those "middle classes" for whose influence supporters and opponents of the government competed both through economic action and through ideological models presented in the mass media.

Table 3
Skill Levels of Active Population

	Thousands of persons	Percentages
Directors, managers, top officials	66.0	2.2
Technical professionals	15.0	0.5
Other professionals with university degrees	39.0	1.3
Technicians on university level	9.0	0.3
Practical technicians	24.0	0.8
Administrative personnel and others of middle level	665.7	22.2
Skilled workers	968.5	32.4
Semiskilled workers	203.9	6.8
Unskilled workers	1,007.5	33.5

But these charts bring out some important facts. One is the great weight of the Chilean working class, which with 46.3 percent of the active population was by far the most numerous social sector. Second is the insignificant number of employers, that is, those who gave the workers jobs (in order to exploit them). Third, the considerable percentage of self-employed—for the most part outside of industry. By way of completing the picture of this sector, 53 percent of the self-employed earned in 1970 a minimum-wage income no higher than an unskilled worker's. We also note that the 22.2 percent for administrative personnel almost coincides with the 24.1 percent for white-collar employees in Table 2. This means that the great majority of persons in the "self-employed" category should be included among the workers in Table 3.

Thus the aggregate of workers, white-collar employees, and self-employed with minimum-wage incomes exceeded 80 percent of Chile's active population. And that coincided with the distribution of national income: over 90 percent of the active population received less than three times the minimum-wage income, and had 45 percent of the total income.

From this we may conclude that while the "middle classes" were a highly important percentage of the population, most of them had common interests with the proletariat and substantial differences with the middle propertied bourgeoisie—i.e., with those 48,000 persons who were 1.6 percent of the economically active population. In the main the "middle classes" were composed of private and public white-collar employees, small peasant proprietors, small merchants, and artisans who employed no one and earned extremely small incomes.

Small and middle industrialists, middle businessmen, and middle landowning farmers formed a minority sector of the "middle classes," with economic and social interests clearly different not only from those of the working class but from those of the other broad strata in the list. At the same time their contradictions with the big bourgeoisie were secondary, since both their conscious objectives and the dynamic of capitalism compelled them to expand their enterprises or lose out and disappear; all their activities tended to imitate and emulate the higher sectors of their class. In his message to Congress on March 4, 1971, President Allende said:

> We must at the same time help the small and middle industrialists, businessmen, and farmers who for many years have been exploited by the big monopolies. Our economic policy guarantees them just treatment. There will be no more financial despoliation, and extortion of the small seller by the big buyer will be stopped. Small and middle industries will have an active role in building the new economy. Taking their place in an apparatus designed to produce more rationally for the majority of Chileans, they will enjoy the support of the social sector. The private, mixed, and social sectors will be precisely delimited.[1]

This line was ratified by the Left leadership, which in the face of the opposition's efforts was always ready to reaffirm its support for small and middle entrepreneurs, as for example at the El Arrayán meeting in February 1972:

> Popular Unity recognizes a legitimate place for the broad strata of small and middle proprietors to exist and develop. We have again and again repeated that the program is not contrary to the interests of the nonmonopolist private sector, which has always had and still has real contradictions with the big monopolistic enterprises of production and distribution.

But these efforts to convince middle proprietors and guarantee their broadest interests collided with their ideological models and potential development goals, for at the same meeting Popular Unity leaders stated:

> However, those objective bases have not so far led to any general understanding nor to forms of systematic cooperation between the government's administrative agencies and the representative bodies of those entrepreneurs. Ideological penetration by reaction has been a stronger force, persuading some of them against their real interests to unite with the big monopolist bourgeoisie in a heterogeneous National Front of the private sector.

In spite of all the concessions that were made, Popular Unity failed to win the confidence of those propertied sectors. It continued to make appeals to components of the "middle classes," making no distinctions between them but considering that all were moved by middle-entrepreneur values.

As evidence of this, the June 1972 report of MAPU, based on the discussion of economic policies that had taken place at the Popular Unity meeting in Lo Curro, said:

> ... from the material standpoint this government has done more than any other for small and middle entrepreneurs. All statistics prove it. . . . For small and middle capitalists the material benefits have kept growing but are not translated into substantial support for the popular government. On the contrary, the monopolist bourgeoisie and its parties and organizations have managed to draw in these sectors against the government.

The fact is that identifying small- and middle-entrepreneur interests with those of the "middle classes" as a whole proved profoundly negative for Popular Unity's policy of alliances. The small and middle capitalists were essentially that—capitalists—and despite their higher-than-ever profits they were frightened by growing popular participation in the country's affairs. They not only wanted immediate profits; even more than that, they wanted those profits guaranteed for the future, and they would not entrust their political representation to such hands, for all of Popular Unity's or the Communist Party's pronouncements. This attempted identification of interests had two consequences. On the one hand, it lightened the ideological task of the big bourgeoisie, who likewise professed common interests with this broad and multi-stratified sector. Thus the models inculcated through decades by education, press, radio and TV, propaganda, and political parties were made to seem threatened by Popular Unity as it sought ever more desperately to convince small and middle capitalists that the reality was otherwise. In other words, Popular Unity's leadership and the government were largely responsible for imposing small- and middle-capitalist models upon those broad strata of public and private white-collar workers, artisans, small merchants, etc., who should have been natural allies of the working class.

On the other hand, middle industrial entrepreneurs never saw Popular Unity as representing them, rightly deeming it impossible to coexist with completely contradictory strategic objectives; so that from the outset they were to be found in Christian Democratic and National party ranks and to a lesser degree in the corporativist movement Patria y Libertad (Fatherland and Liberty). Thus this social sector, to which Popular Unity tirelessly appealed, found its natural political home with those who defended capitalism not only then but for the future.

The result was that to implement its policy of alliance with the "middle classes" Popular Unity had to reach out beyond its own constituency, particularly to Christian Democracy. That is, the vagueness of the term "middle classes," its generalized identification with the values of the predominant sector of the middle industrial bourgeoisie, had the effect of pushing toward that capitalist sector's models other strata which should have identified with the government. In opening a dialogue with Christian Democracy and recognizing that party as representative of the "middle classes"—that is, of small and middle entrepreneurs—Popular Unity in effect broadened Christian Democratic ranks with a heterogeneous assortment of other sectors of the population.

Clearly this was not a matter of "errors" by Popular Unity but of the prevalence within it of the tendency basically inspired by the Communist Party, responding to that party's concept of the "National Liberation Front."

The policy imposed by the Communist Party was protested by the tendencies that rightly considered Popular Unity's tactical postulates as subject to the development of a revolutionary strategy for beginning to build socialism. Against the government's vacillations and conciliations, the Socialist Party, whose adherents included a strong force of radicalized workers and *pobladores,* demanded an aggressive and sustained anticapitalist policy. As Carlos Altamirano put it, speaking about alliances:

> We Socialists don't believe the middle strata can be bought with flattery, with promises of a living standard that is often impossible to maintain in our impoverished countries, or with legislation to provide them with special benefits. Historically the middle strata have sided with the victorious class. It is the strength and energy of the popular government that will either draw them to us or throw them into the arms of reaction."[2]

The Socialist rejection of the agreements with Christian Democracy coherently expressed that position, but was never applied by Popular Unity, to whose general line the Socialist Party always ended by submitting. In any case, Altamirano's analysis also committed the error of abstractly treating the "middle classes" as a single entity.

Especially significant was the Communist Party's effort, at the June 1972 Lo Curro meeting when Popular Unity leaders foregathered with President Allende, to find a platform substantially acceptable to the middle bourgeoisie—the "national bourgeoisie," as that party called it.

On that occasion, while there was more stress on consolidating the revolutionary process, the policy followed up until then was reaffirmed. That is, a policy of consolidating the gains achieved in implementing the program; determining in agreement with Christian Democracy which and how many enterprises should definitely pass into the Social Production Sector; halting inflation by a series of technical measures implying "efficiency in state enterprise administration" (cutting down personnel and increasing production); and reducing currency in circulation by limiting wages and salaries. Responsible for all this would be a new ministerial team whose outstanding feature was the departure of Pedro Vuskovic, the finance minister who had pressed for immediate establishment of the Social Production Sector.

This policy of generating confidence in important sectors of the propertied class was complemented by discussions aimed at reaching basic agreements with Christian Democracy, then led by its "progressive" wing. The talks broke down at the last minute due to pressure from ex-President Frei, the significance of which will be seen later. What is important to note is the Communist Party's determination that such agreements with the middle bourgeoisie were absolutely indispensable. As its Political Commission member Volodia Teitelboim said:

> Our idea is to continue seeking unity of all Chileans who favor structural changes and opening the road to a new society. . . . For if in fact we did reach virtual agreements—broken though they were at the last minute—about problems of prime importance which always made progress more likely in achieving whatever Popular Unity's and Radomiro Tomic's[3] programs have in common . . . that in our view is not a gratuitous fact but a reflection of a deep necessity of Chilean society, a necessity that still awaits fulfillment, since it is a historical imperative.[4]

Repeatedly throughout the process Popular Unity committed the error of seeing a basic mutual contradiction between the big and the middle bourgeoisie, overestimating the differences and attempting to win an important part of the latter for a policy of thoroughgoing transformations. The repeated failure of these efforts shows, on the one hand, the two groups' essential unity of interest in the survival of a society led by the bourgeoisie as a class, and on the other, profound requirements imposed by the needs of capitalist development. (This will be dealt with further on.)

Included in this error of overall analysis were the importance attributed to purely economic measures and the lack of an adequate ideological policy, which led to the projection of models favorable to the "middle classes"—i.e., the small and middle propertied bourgeoisie—in pro-government media. Apart from some Quimantú publications, the magazines, dailies, radio, and TV controlled by Popular Unity propagated values and goals that were neither those of the working class nor those of a society in transition to socialism. Thus the big bourgeoisie's ideological dominance over wide sectors of Chilean society was further affirmed.

The policy that the Communist Party could never implement was thus plainly defined by Orlando Millas of that party's Central Committee at a Party Plenum on October 4, 1971: "To deprive sedition of its chief base of support, and to assure democratic development, it is of prime importance to resolve in the people's favor the struggle with the financial oligarchy; this requires organic adjustment and delimitation of the social sector of the economy so as to avoid unjustified fears on the part of middle and small industrialists."[5]

Meanwhile the Communist-oriented tendency was sharply criticizing the revolutionary positions with which it coexisted in Popular Unity, seeking at once to disarm these ideologically and to win the "national bourgeoisie's" support by reducing the contradictions into a struggle between the people and the financial oligarchy. In the October 1971 issue of *Finanzas Públicas,* organ of the Office of the Budget, whose editors definitely followed the Communist Party line, appeared the following:

> The working class is vitally interested in allies on other rungs of the social ladder. If it lets itself be isolated, its hegemony will not be possible. Great harm has been done by those who in an opportunistic scramble have thought it easier to advocate incorporating any and all enterprises into the social sector without rhyme or reason, instead of maintaining coordinated and effective trade-union, social, political, economic, and administrative action to ensure the workers' rights and persuade entrepreneurs to increase production, thus helping to stop speculation and sabotage.

Obviously this program had small chance of acceptance by most of the Socialist Party, by MAPU, or by the forces outside Popular Unity, like MIR, since their basic membership consisted precisely of small- and middle-industry workers who found it quite impossible to curb their fellow-workers' demands and "win" the bosses for "increased production." For these political sectors the Chilean process was an uninterrupted march toward socialism which had to be consistently anticapitalist in content, not merely antioligarchic.

The result was that despite the predominance within Popular Unity of Communist Party conceptions—which virtually replaced all others after the Lo Curro meeting with Millas's installation as finance minister—there was no coherence among the popular forces; the small and middle entrepreneurs' response was obstinately negative, and important working-class sectors were demobilized.

This last needs statistical substantiation to bring out its great importance.

Today the Social Production Sector represents only 20 percent of production and somewhat less than 20 percent of the labor force—figures that would rise to around 30 percent if all ninety of the monopoly enterprises scheduled to be statified according to the program were included. This means that some 10,000 enterprises with more than five workers, and 20,000 or 25,000 semi-artisan or artisan units—respectively employing 300,000 and about 80,000 persons—remain in the Private Property Sector. In contrast, there are some 150,000 workers in the Social Production Sector. The proportions remaining in private hands is even greater in the commercial sector than in the industrial sector.[6]

What this signifies is that the policies promoted by the Communist Party within the government did not provide class objectives capable of mobilizing that enormous segment of industrial workers who were the main body of the urban proletariat. Those 300,000 workers, more than 50 percent of the industrial working class, were in small and middle enterprises where they were expected to function efficiently in alliance with their employers. Lack of a social and political program for this great sector of workers brought negative results for Popular Unity, and had the effect of making penetration by Christian Democratic influence that much easier. And this the CUT election results—a surprise never explained by Popular Unity leaders—would confirm.

Founded in 1953 and with slightly more than 800,000 members, CUT had by 1972 recruited into Chile's major union organization only 25 percent of the active working population and probably only 10 percent of the wage-earning peasantry. The difficulties imposed by prevailing legislation, and the traditional hostility of successive governments since 1953 (which never recognized CUT's legal existence), as well as CUT's bureaucratic structures, explain this low membership. Nevertheless, CUT had won legal representation of the workers in tough battles; and in May 1972, when its leadership was for the first time elected by universal and secret vote, all political tendencies with popular representation, organized in unions of workers, white-collar employees, and campesinos, took part.

The results were announced only after sixty days and were the target of repeated complaints by Socialists and Christian Democrats. Popular Unity parties won 68.8 percent, Christian Democrats and "independents" (a mask for the National Party) 27.6 percent, MIR (with Christian Left support) 1.8 percent, Popular Socialist Union (left splinter from the Socialist Party) 1 percent, Revolutionary Communist Party (Maoist splinter from the Communist Party) 0.7 percent. That is, forces opposing the program pushed by Popular Unity won more than a quarter of the organized workers' votes. This was proof that the policy of alliances with the "middle classes" neither yielded the hoped-for fruits in that sector nor helped to win over important sectors of workers and campesinos who, finding no action program to transform existing relations within small and middle private industry and agriculture, fell under the influence of Christian Democratic union leaders.

1. Cited in *El Pensamiento económico del Gobierno de Allende* (Santiago de Chile: Editorial Universitaria, 1971).
2. Carlos Altamirano, *Decisión Revolucionaria* (Santiago de Chile: Quimantú, 1973).
3. Christian Democratic presidential candidate in September 1970. (trans.)
4. Quoted in the Communist daily *El Siglo* (Santiago de Chile), June 15, 1972.
5. *Documentos Políticos* magazine (Bogotá, Colombia), August 1972.
6. Alberto Martínez, in *Chile Hoy* magazine (Santiago de Chile), September 1, 1972.

PRINCIPAL POLITICAL ORGANIZATIONS IN CHILE, 1972

	Origins	Ideology
Movement of the Revolutionary Left (MIR)	Coalition of several revolutionary groups in 1965, student struggles, rejection of traditional workers' parties	Marxist-Leninist, strong influence of Che Guevara, to lesser extent of Trotskyism
Socialist Party of Chile (PS)	Alliance of Marxist intellectuals (including leftist PC dissidents and Progressive Masons) in 1933	Marxist with Trotskyist and social-democratic tendencies. Anti-imperialist. Later, Leninist tendencies
Communist Party of Chile (PC)	Transformation in 1922 of Socialist Workers Party into section of Third International, with base in labor unions	Marxist with Stalinist development accentuated by influence of popular-front line
Christian Democratic Party (DC)	Started 1938 as "Falange" by Conservative Party youth, based on Catholic intellectuals and professionals	Liberal, influenced by Jacques Maritain and papal encyclicals; "communitarian" alternative to capitalism and communism
National Party (PN)	Fusion (1966) of Conservative and Liberal parties both dating from first half of 19th century	Manchester liberal with conservative influences and authoritarian tendencies
Patria y Libertad Nationalist Movement (MNPL)	Started 1970 as reply to popular government by petty-bourgeois followers of Jorge Alessandri	Nationalist, reactionary, antipopular, corporativist and fascist tendencies
Radical Party (PR)	Started in last quarter 19th century by Masonic mining, professional and government employee sectors	Bourgeois, secular reformism with strong Masonic influence
Radical Democracy and Radical Left Party		

Leaders' Background	Electoral Strength April 1971	Electoral Strength March 1973	Classes and Social Sectors Supporting
University-educated petty-bourgeois	Not participating	Supported PS	Students, campesinos (esp. indigenous areas), *pobladores*; to a lesser extent, small and middle industry workers
Petty-bourgeois professionals with worker/campesino cadres	22.38%	18.66%	Blue- and white-collar workers, campesinos, *pobladores*, students, propertyless petty bourgeoisie
Workers, petty-bourgeois professionals; leadership based on professional party officials	16.97%	16.22%	Blue- and white-collar workers, students, petty bourgeoisie, *pobladores*, campesinos
Intellectuals and professionals linked to local oligarchy, middle industrial entrepreneurs	25.62%	29.12%	Industrial, commercial, financial bourgeoisie, petty and middle bourgeoisie, *pobladores*, students, campesinos, blue- and white-collar workers
Remnants of agrarian oligarchy, big entrepreneurs linked to U.S. concerns	18.12%	21.31%	Agrarian, financial, industrial, merchant bourgeoisie, petty and middle bourgeoisie, students
Petty-bourgeois professionals, remnant of oligarchy	Not participating	Supported PN	Agrarian bourgeoisie, petty- and middle-bourgeois professionals, students
Petty-bourgeois professionals, government, employees, businessmen	8.00%	3.72%	Public and private white-collar workers, small merchants
Small and middle agrarian and industrial bourgeoisie	3.83%	4.07%	Middle and small agrarian and commercial bourgeoisie

	Short-term Program	Methods of Struggle	Trade-union Strength (CUT, 1972)
Movement of the Revolutionary Left (MIR)	Socialism, popular power, dictatorship of proletariat	Direct action, armed struggle (*foco* insurrection), rejection of institutional/electoral mechanisms	1.8%
Socialist Party of Chile (PS)	Popular Unity program, beginning construction of socialism, development of popular power	Parliamentary action, support of government, rejection of inevitable armed struggle, mass actions	27.5%
Communist Party of Chile (PC)	Popular Unity program with full guarantees to nonmonopolist bourgeoisie; an "advanced society"	Parliamentary action, support of government, full respect for established institutionality, mass demonstrations	29.5%
Christian Democratic Party (DC)	Defense of "middle classes," opposition to government, "national reconstruction"	Parliamentary obstruction, alliance with extreme Right, blackmail of government, coup d'état	26.0%
National Party (PN)	Defense of employer guilds, "civil resistance," "national reconstruction"	Parliamentary obstruction, alliance with DC, economic sabotage, coup d'état	—
Patria y Libertad Nationalist Movement (MNPL)	"Integrated" society with entrepreneurial guilds, parties of "order" and armed forces	Sabotage, street disturbances, coup d'état	—
Radical Party (PR)	Popular Unity program with guarantees to private property	Parliamentary action, support of government	6.0%
Radical Democracy and Radical Left Party	Defense of "middle classes," "national reconstruction"	Removal of president, coup d'état	—

3 THE ECONOMIC PROGRAM AND LAWS OF THE MARKET

The characteristics of Chile as a capitalist, monoproductive, dependent country, with increasing monopolization of basic production and an extremely low and stagnant rate of investment, became even more marked in the 1960s.

As a consequence of the concentration of capital, 3.2 percent of the earning population in 1968 received 42 percent of the national income and 47 percent received only 12 percent; 45 percent of national income went to 90 percent of the active employed population.

Three percent of industrial enterprises, with 58 percent of the capital and 52 percent of the gross surpluses, produced 51 percent of total industrial values. The financial concentration was also striking: in 1969, 0.4 percent of debtors held 25 percent of banking credit. Average production growth between 1967 and 1970 was 2.7 percent below the average for Latin America as a whole, which was growing at a rate of 5 percent a year. Inflation for 1968, 1969, and 1970 was 28, 29, and 35 percent respectively, the rate steadily growing. Unemployment moved in the same direction, with 4.9, 5, and 6 percent respectively. Contributing to this was a foreign debt which, from $1,869 billion in 1964, reached $3,866 billion under the Frei administration in 1970—the highest per capita in the world.[1]

On top of all this, Chile's main resources were in the hands of international capital, which devoted itself to the exploitation of mines, industries, and services, in addition to its involvement in the money market and foreign trade. In 1967 the hard-currency outflow in revenue to foreign capital reached $201 million, i.e., 20 percent of that year's hard-currency inflow.[2] In 1968, sixty-one of the one hundred largest industrial enterprises had foreign participation and in forty of them it was predominant.[3]

Chile in 1970 was indeed far from being a country "in process of development," and continuation of the same policies held out no hope of change in either the short or the long term.

The basic program of Popular Unity, resolutely put into effect in the first year after November 4, 1970, attempted to achieve a profound transformation of existing relations by applying the following substantive measures:

The new economy will consist of three basic sectors: social, mixed, and private property. The economic transformation process starts with setting up a predominant state sector comprising enterprises now owned by the state and those to be expropriated. First to be nationalized will be those basic resources, such as copper, iron, nitrate, and other mines, which are now owned by foreign capital and domestic monopolies. Thus the following will become part of this nationalized sector:

1. The big copper, nitrate, iodine, iron, and coal-mining companies.

2. The country's financial system, especially private banks and insurance companies.

3. Foreign trade.

4. The big distributive enterprises and monopolies.

5. The strategic industrial monopolies.

6. In general, those activities that determine the country's economic and social development, such as production and distribution of electrical power and rail, air, and maritime transport; communications; production, refining, and distribution of petroleum and its derivatives, including natural gas; steel; cement; petrochemicals and industrial chemicals; cellulose; paper.

There will be a mixed sector comprising enterprises with combined state and private capital.

The Private Property Sector will embrace areas of industry, mining, agriculture, and services where the means of production continue to be privately owned. Numerically these will be the majority of enterprises.

Agrarian reform will be accelerated by expropriation of holdings above the established maximum (the equivalent of eighty irrigated hectares) according to conditions in the various zones. Expropriated lands will where possible be organized as cooperatives.

We note that the measures tending to transform the economic structure pointed in three basic directions: nationalization of foreign-owned mineral wealth; creation of a new extractive-industrial-financial-commercial state sector to become the driving force of development and make it possible to direct and plan the whole economy; extension of the already-begun agrarian reform to eliminate all holdings above the equivalent of eighty irrigated hectares.

Thus the program posed an immediate threat of expropriation to imperialist interests and to the big industrial, financial, commercial, and agrarian bourgeoisie, while respecting and guaranteeing the small and middle bourgeoisie's property in all those areas.

To overcome economic stagnation in conformity with these property transformations, the program attempted to implement a policy of stimulation and development based on these points:

> Resolve the immediate problems of the masses. Guarantee adequately paid jobs to all Chileans of working age. Free Chile from subjection to foreign capital. Assure such rapid and decentralized economic growth as will develop productive forces to the utmost. Implement a foreign-trade policy that will develop and diversify our exports. Take all measures conducive to monetary stability.

Here we note that the proposed transformations aimed at ending the domination of multinational enterprises of finance capital, of certain big industrial monopolies, and of the latifundia, so as to free the productive forces from the main obstacles to rapid and sustained expansion. This program was to be implemented by the state, which would replace a big bourgeoisie too weak and too deeply involved with foreign interests to do the job. Therefore the projected economic policy sought to be congruent with the hoped-for class alliance, by leaving management of the majority of enterprises in the hands of private owners who would recognize that the expansion of demand in cities and countryside favored their interests, and that their management would be facilitated by the support of government agencies within a national economic context that would end their subjection to big multinational concerns.

However, on this level, too, the program was full of ambiguity, since it saw the period of carrying out these measures as "a necessary stage for the building of socialism"—that is, as part of a strategy leading to a new and qualitatively different society. The two coexisting lines in Popular Unity emerged also on the economic level, for one sector aimed to apply the anti-imperialist and antioligarchic measures from a long-range political perspective, while the other saw them as merely a tactical step in an uninterrupted march toward socialism. Both concepts of the economic program had their parallels in their respective class-alliance policies.

Over a long period of Popular Unity administration, lasting at least until early 1972, these basic divergences faded, in view of the existing consensus in implementing the program, with greater or lesser speed and thoroughness. Let us examine this process.

During most of this century copper, mainly exploited by two big U.S. companies, has been the principal wealth of Chile. That exploitation is a typical example of plunder of a dependent country's resources, these companies having "exported" from Chile in the form of profits about $3 billion from a net investment of some $750 million. The significance of these figures emerges from the fact that in 1970 Chile's national capital was $10 billion; that is, U.S. copper companies alone had taken out to that point a third of all that Chile had been able to accumulate in its territory since it ceased to be a Spanish colony more than 150 years ago.

Furthermore, the copper companies belong to financial groups owning copper-processing enterprises in the United States, so that it is in their interest to take out the copper at the lowest possible price. During World War II the price was set at 11.5 cents (U.S.) per pound even though copper was quoted much higher in the London market. This was justified as Chile's "contribution" to the fight against the Axis powers. Under similar conditions the price was set at 24.5 cents in the Korean War period and at 36 cents during the imperialist invasion of Vietnam, when the London metals-market quotation was 60 cents. These price jugglings were permitted and protected by every government that Chile endured up to that time, including in particular the

Popular Front—Radical administration (1938-1948) and the administrations of Gen. Carlos Ibañez (1952-1958) and of Christian Democrat Frei (1964-1970). But that did not prevent the U.S. concerns from garnering the huge profits to which we have referred, higher than what they obtained from mines they owned elsewhere in the world. Thus Anaconda, owner of Chile's Chuquicamata, El Salvador, and Potrerillos mines, in 1955–1970 earned a world profit average of 3.67 percent while its Chilean profits rose to 21.51 percent; Kennecott, with a world average of 9.95 percent, earned 52.87 percent on its Chilean business.

President Allende proposed, in view of these precedents, to recover the ores in Chilean soil and their installations by buying the U.S. enterprises at book value, from which would be deducted the total profits exceeding 10 percent per year on the book value. This was an anti-imperialist redemption policy that could have deep repercussions for the properties of every big multinational firm operating in the entire so-called Third World.

Once again, consistent with the characteristics of the Chilean process, this was carried out by a proposed constitutional amendment that stipulated the following:

(c) Insert the following new paragraph between the present paragraphs 5 and 6: "In the case of nationalization of mining activities or enterprises in the legal category of Big Mining [those companies that mine more than 75,000 metric tons of copper ore per year], the nationalization may embrace the enterprises themselves, rights in them, or all or part of their assets. The nationalization may also extend to the assets of third parties of any type directly and necessarily involved in said activities or enterprises. The amount of indemnity or indemnities payable, which will vary according to circumstances, may be determined on the basis of the original cost of said assets minus amortizations, depreciations, cost reductions, and devaluations due to obsolescence. All or part of the excess profits obtained by the nationalized enterprises may be deducted from the indemnity. Indemnities will be payable in cash unless the party concerned accepts payment in another form, over a period not exceeding thirty years and under the conditions determined by law. The state may take material possession of assets included in the nationalization immediately after this goes into effect."

The big U.S. companies' 1955–1970 profits in excess of 10 percent proved to be larger than the book value of their net investments to date. The enterprises were in debt to the Chilean state.

The policy of reclaiming natural assets which was advocated and implemented by the Allende government, went well beyond Chilean frontiers: the "excess profits" thesis was a dangerous precedent for imperialism, which circumstances prevented it from responding to with armed invasion as had been its practice for decades, especially in Latin America. Instead it embarked on a policy of pressure and economic blockade on many levels: cancellation of loans, credits, and investments by financial agencies under U.S. government influence as well as by private concerns; stiffened terms for servicing the external debt; and demands on Western Europe to embargo copper shipments. The effect on the balance of payments was brutal, as Table 4 shows:

TABLE 4

In millions of dollars

Year	Trade balance	Current balance	Net capital inflow	Errors and omissions	Balance of payments
1967	111.5	-127.4	123.9	-21.5	-25.0
1968	119.7	-135.3	303.5	-41.2	127.0
1969	252.9	-5.6	238.2	—	232.6
1970	62.1	-57.4	148.5	—	91.1
1971	—	-211.5	-99.7	—	-311.2

Source: Central Bank of Chile.

This meant that numerous previously approved projects which were in the works had to be suspended, especially middle- and long-term investment plans.

Renegotiation of the foreign debt with Chile's creditors in the "Club de Paris" consortium was a long and difficult process in which the creditors imposed measures of a traditionally regressive kind. As the Chilean delegates said, "The policy of the iron heel is being applied to Chile." A "standby" was finally conceded consisting of facilities and extensions which maintained the situation as a permanent threat in the event that Chile had to default on its debt, and which made any long-term investment plans impossible.

Coinciding in October 1972 with a great reactionary offensive by the bourgeoisie inside Chile, Kennecott demanded in the French courts an embargo on a copper shipment then due at Le Havre, and soon afterward Anaconda took similar action. These maneuvers were not entirely successful but nonetheless had a negative effect on Chilean exports, maintaining the threat of legal action by U.S. concerns anywhere in the world at any moment.

Nationalization of the copper mines did not raise revenue to the hoped-for extent, mainly due to falling copper prices in international markets during most of the period but also to sabotage of production which prevented fulfillment of plans. But this in no way diminishes the profound significance of a national and anti-imperialist policy which, over a sufficient period, should have enabled hard-currency inflow to become the pillar of Chile's investment programs. On the ideological level the nationalization was highly favorable to the popular government, both because of the mechanisms used to carry it out and because of the sense of unity and dignity it instilled in the working masses—a spirit that was maintained through other measures that aimed to reduce the Chilean economy's traditional dependency on foreign and especially U.S. capital.

In the year 1932 Chile had lived through a rare experience. On June 4 of that year a military group seized power, proclaiming a Socialist Republic of Chile which lasted only thirteen days, to be overthrown by another military coup restoring "order." Those events left behind a series of legends, the glow of an unattainable utopia that had been snatched from hands already grasping it. Nearly forty years later it was realized that legends were not all that remained. There was also a Decree-Law No. 520, promulgated under the Socialist Republic and never repealed, which authorized state intervention of any industry that was threatened with bankruptcy or had problems deriving from social conflicts. The process initiated by Popular Unity called for setting up the Social Production Sector by combining mobilization of the masses with utilization of prevailing legislation. Social conflicts were breaking out in precisely those enterprises that the program envisaged for inclusion in the social sector, and in that process the industrial working class was involved and committed. Thus, with the workers' effective participation, the state sector of the economy began to grow as the initial interventions were followed by expropriation of some enterprises and acquisition of others.

During 1971 most textile, metallurgical, cement, fishing, and domestic electrical enterprises, the beer monopoly, the big publishing house Quimantú—seventy industrial enterprises in all—became part of the social production complex. These, together with the nationalized copper, iron, nitrate, and coal concerns, and sixteen banks, acquisition of whose stocks permitted the executive to control 90 percent of credit—and with the initial state sector of petroleum, railroads, airlines, electricity, steel, etc.—put planning agencies in a position to structure a development program based on the government's plans.

The Social Production Sector was not created without overcoming—partially and temporarily—the resistance of the bourgeoisie and the state institutions it controlled. Its creation was essentially achieved by the workers' mobilization and by the resoluteness, in that period, of the ministry of the economy charged with implementing it.

But on June 29, 1971, the office of the comptroller of the Republic declined to certify the requisition order on Manufactura Yarur, SA, one of the largest textile consortia with a monopoly of various products: "The occupation of an industry, constituting as it does a punishable offense, does not authorize nor make viable the requisition of the establishments in question." The rejection of measures to build the Social Production Sector showed, at this early stage, how legal mechanisms could obstruct such measures. And this was to be confirmed by the comptroller's systematic defense of employer interests throughout 1971, and through rejection of all demands for requisitions, to which the workers responded with new demonstrations. On September 8 the National Party presented the first constitutional charge against the minister of the economy, Pedro Vuskovic, insisting that the requisitions he ordered "are illegal and constitute a flagrant violation of our Constitution and prevailing laws."

Despite resistance, by the beginning of 1972 the government had succeeded in solidly advancing this part of the program and acquiring the necessary tools to energize national production and speed its growth.

An especially important aspect of the building of the Social Production Sector was the workers' participation in state enterprises as members of their Administrative Councils. The workers' traditional relations of dependence within the production process were thus profoundly changed. In line with the CUT-government accord, all Administrative Councils now had five members and a chairperson named by the government and five workers' representatives elected by universal and secret ballot. These councils resolved all problems of the enterprise within the general lines laid down by CORFO (Promotion and Development Corporation) and were empowered to make decisions on all levels: production, pay scales, investments, contracts—everything was decided with the workers' participation in the council of each enterprise. At the same time, the government-designated officials were almost all members of Popular Unity parties, resulting in even closer relations and interaction between them and Social Production Sector workers. When the first bourgeois insurrection occurred in October 1972, these officials were the most enthusiastic and resolute defenders of popular conquests.

Agrarian reform was speeded by application of the law passed in the Frei period which provided for possible expropriation of all rural properties in excess of the equivalent of eighty irrigated hectares, with indemnity for the owner, who could also retain an area of his choice up to the maximum, along with its buildings, machinery, tools, and animals. The prevailing law consequently affected the interests of the surviving Chilean oligarchy and also gave rise to a middle agrarian bourgeoisie which became the most powerful force in the countryside. To push agrarian reform, large amounts of capital for payment of indemnities became and absolute necessity.

Land expropriation continued through 1971, as in the Frei period, but thousands of farms nonetheless remained in their old owners' hands. In these circumstances the campesino movement reached new levels of struggle, spearheaded principally by the agricultural semi-proletariat—farmworkers and sharecroppers—who carried out 1,278 land "takeovers" during that year. Thus agrarian reform moved into higher gear and by mid-1972 latifundia were essentially eliminated, but not without fierce daily class struggle. The fact is that while the law gave land to large sectors of landless campesinos, in the main to be worked cooperatively, the eighty-hectare equivalent which the old owner could keep—along with the machinery, animals, capital, and commercial relations that were still his—put him in a position to continue dominating property relations in some rural areas. The agrarian reform was given impetus by vast strata of poor campesinos as their level of conscious-ness and organization grew, encouraged both by leftist officials of the agrarian agencies and by regional leaders of some popular parties. But from the end of 1971, the two divergent lines within Popular Unity, resulting from the enormous difficulties of making the proposed class alliance a reality, came into confrontation in the countryside. By mid-1972 the rural class war extended throughout the center and south of Chile, and farm production fell in consequence of this and of landowner resistance in the form of contraband sales to Argentina, sabotage, and armed violence.

At the February 1972 meeting in El Arrayán, Popular Unity's National Committee could report enthusiastically on the advance of the program:

> Great victories were won in the battle of production during 1971. In the year of copper nationalization Chile produced 750,000 tons, 40,000 more than in 1970 (6 percent increase). . . . Some 100,000 housing units went into construction in 1971, an un-precedented figure that will mean solving the housing problem of more than 300,000 persons. . . . These successes have given jobs to 200,000 new workers. Today 3,140,000 Chileans have paid employment. . . . 1,378 latifundios comprising almost 2,600,000 hectares were expropriated, the equivalent of all the previous government's expropriations in six years. . . . At the same time an almost 9 percent growth in the national product, and some 13 percent in industrial production, were achieved. The unemploy-ment rate fell from 8.3 to 3.8 percent. Real income rose by 20 percent and the wage-earners' consumption level by 13 percent, so that blue- and white-collar workers now receive 60 percent of the national income as against 51 percent previously. Price rises were substantially lower than in 1970.[4]

These optimistic figures did not blind the National Committee to the existence of more dangerous factors, though their full significance was not seen:

> Wage adjustments went beyond what had been anticipated. Due to the nonpayment of dividends owed by the copper concerns, the sharp reduction of external credit lines, and the drastic drop in copper prices, reserve funds had to be used for paying

previous debts while imports increased by 9.6 percent relative to 1970. These factors also led to shortages of certain products, although consumption levels were appreciably higher than in that year.[5]

This last encompasses most of the problems that were subsequently to put Chile's economy out of joint: the pressure from abroad that shut off an important source of income and reduced hard-currency inflow, the increase of imports not under the government's control, and the incipient shortages of some imported goods, mainly raw materials and spare parts. The El Arrayán document added:

Reactivation of the economy has inevitably led to enhanced utilization of productive capacity, which imposes real limitations on new expansion of consumption and makes urgent the necessity of increasing investments. The massive accumulation of liquidity in the system limits the flexibility of financial policy and makes stricter and more selective management indispensable.

From this analysis, though it was less than a full one of the problems faced, conclusions could be drawn pointing to exhaustion of the equilibrium implicit in the government's economic development model. Popular Unity's technicians were not unaware of this but the outcome was a kind of compromise. On the one hand, it was agreed to speed up the creation of the Social Production Sector in order to weaken the power of reaction in certain monopolies and its access to large financial resources. At the same time guarantees were reiterated to "broad strata of interests in the nonmonopolistic sector"—that is, to middle industrial, agricultural, and commercial entrepreneurs.

What was happening to the Chilean economy? The capitalist system is based on the activity of private entrepreneurs who obtain a certain margin of profit on their invested capital (higher in the case of monopolies); and that margin was increased by the government's policy of augmenting demand and hence making possible a faster turnover of capital. But as was noted with concern in February 1972, the demand for more goods and services was not accompanied by significantly higher production (apparently the ministry of the economy technicians overestimated the capacity of idle production units), and this produced strong pressure on prices. There were secondary factors of some importance: smuggling of goods to neighboring countries, especially Argentina and Peru; taking advantage of the high value of the U.S. dollar on Chile's black market and Chile's lower production costs; and the speculative stockpiling practiced by industrialists and businessmen. But the main factor was the failure of production to grow in accordance with the real needs of the program.

This situation was beyond the government's control since the Social Production Sector was far from able to supply the most pressing needs for products (it was in any case primarily concentrated in basic sectors supplying raw materials and cheap semiprocessed products to middle and small industry). Only two roads remained open: either greatly increased investment to ensure fast growth of supply, or managed reduction of consumption at the other end of the chain.

Traditionally in Chile the state was the biggest investor but, as we have seen, investment had been almost stagnant in recent years. The situation did not improve under the Popular Unity government. On the contrary. Income from exports, mainly copper, failed to come up to expectations since the world price fell to 50 cents (U.S.) a pound. Foreign credits, always one of the chief sources, fell off to such an extent as to produce along with the former factor a $300 million deficit in the balance of payments. Thus to obtain investment funds the government had no other recourse than drastic redefinition of its tax policy by heavy exactions on the small and middle bourgeoisie's profits. But this meant an abrupt turn of the rudder in the government's whole concept of changes to be made.

Investments in the private sector did not materialize either, and the government had no legal tools with which to force them. The middle and small bourgeoisie were, after all, not merely producers but consumers: they wanted to use their high profits to satisfy their cravings for cars, houses, and luxury items. More important, they wanted "security" in the face of political instability, and to get it they invested their profits in black-market dollars, which paid off up to forty times the bank exchange rate, which was restricted to import operations. So investments were not forthcoming to the extent necessary, either from the state or from private entrepreneurs.

Management of consumption was even more difficult. We have seen that Popular Unity, based on the alliance with the "middle classes," did not modify its ideological models as these were set forth in pro-government media. Now the weakness of its political and economic muscle became dramatically evident. It was in no position to suppress the sale of certain products which the opposition insisted on having as an inherent right under a democratic system; and there was a growing psychosis created .by genuine scarcities and whipped up by right-wing media. By mid-1972 it had become manifestly impossible, within institutional channels, to increase the masses' buying power to any substantial extent and at the same time develop the market economy.

Once again Popular Unity's two central tendencies came into acute contradiction with respect to how the situation might be resolved.

In his book *Chile, Una Economía en Transición,* Sergio Ramos had this to say about the role of the small and middle propertied bourgeoisie:

> An economy like Chile's, with so many small- and middle-capitalist producers exploited and dominated by big monopolies . . . generates at least two very important conditions: first, from the standpoint of their objective interests as capitalists, the elimination of private monopolistic concentration and the creation of a new dynamism of economic growth open much more favorable conditions for them, since rapid and enduring increase of production and productivity must be a prime objective of the new system. Second, from the broader standpoint of the economy as a whole, the new production-distribution articulation around a dominant state sector and the need to accelerate economic growth require retention of the economy's private sector, which due to its size and complexity, cannot be suddenly replaced by socialized enterprises.

Contradictions have indeed always existed between different sectors of the bourgeoisie, especially between the monopolist sector allied to imperialist interests and other sectors. But the distinction must be made between principal and secondary contradictions. We may all agree that the whole private sector cannot be "suddenly" replaced by socialized enterprises, but when a social revolutionary process is under way the threatened classes are moved not only by their present interests but especially by their concern to survive as a class. Thus a short- or medium-term alliance was not enough for the middle entrepreneurs, and they minimized their differences with the big bourgeoisie in the face of the main contradiction with the workers and the program of "beginning the construction of socialism." This is clearly a problem of the realities of power, since a government in effective possession of the necessary mechanisms and resources will not immediately undertake to socialize the whole economy, but will be in a position to control supply and demand as well as small- and middle-bourgeois investments and savings. That was of course not the case here, and the envisioned growth of "production and productivity" under the anticipated favorable conditions did not materialize.

Already in October 1971 the left wing of the Socialist Party was impugning the abovementioned tendencies:

> Furthermore, this conservative option [to consolidate past gains] clearly commits the economistic error of placing the economic imperative "production, for example" ahead of the political imperative "power," and that at a point when hegemony has not yet been consolidated. This was not the case with the Soviet NEP in 1921, when Lenin called for consolidation and recovery of production levels diminished during the civil war, but only *after* that war had been won.[6]

In mid-1972 the economic situation was characterized by accelerating inflation (over 100 percent a year) and a general scarcity of consumer goods and spare parts. It was then that the Lo Curro meeting took place, where the two divergent lines confronted each other, with MAPU speaking up most lucidly for the revolutionary Left's policy of deepening the process, speeding the growth of the social sector, discriminating in production and imports in the wage-earners' favor, pushing a price, wage, and tax policy that would hurt the bourgeoisie, government and worker control of key private enterprises, development of the JAP control agencies (Juntas de Abastecimiento y Precios—Supply and Price Committees), and other measures.

The line pushed by the Communist Party proposed in essence to "consolidate" the process, that is, to stop at the stage already reached, extending new long-term guarantees to the "middle classes." It consisted of strategic reordering of the tactical program on the economic level, which meant finding formulas of agreement with the middle bourgeoisie's chief political spokesman, Christian Democracy. The Communist line was totally victorious at the Popular Unity meeting with President Allende at Lo Curro, and Communist Orlando Millas was named finance minister.

From that time—mid-June 1972—until the coup d'état fifteen months later, this economic line was applied, in a setting of intensified inflation, shortages, and dismemberment of the mechanisms linking production and distribution. And small and middle entrepreneurs not only remained unconvinced that investments should be made to increase production, but along with other big-bourgeois sectors turned many of their assets to speculation, thus heightening the shortages of popular consumer goods and contributing to the inflation that plagued the country.

Chile thus resembled a ship in a storm trying to sail in one direction—the alliance with the "middle classes"—and blown in the other, violently rocked by those same presumptive "allies."

During 1973 the economy was to deteriorate precipitously, and the possible roads to follow were deeply antagonistic: stability, recovery, and development could only be achieved by superexploitation of wage workers or by expropriation of the bourgeoisie, big and middle. There were no other alternatives. The laws of the capitalist market could not be twisted with promises and vows of good behavior.

1. National Planning Office, Santiago, 1971.
2. Ibid.
3. Ibid.
4. *Conclusiones de la Reunión del Comité Nacional de la UP*, February 1972.
5. Ibid.
6. *Indoamérica* magazine (Santiago de Chile), No. 6, May 1971.

4 DEVELOPMENT
   OF THE CLASS STRUGGLE

> We want it very clearly understood that public order on the one
> hand, and a new social order on the other, are two different
> things. Public order is governed by juridical and legal norms. The
> social order implies material realities, class positions, confronta-
> tion between different interests. The government over which I
> preside is the product of efforts by the popular masses. We have
> maintained public order because that is our obligation. We will
> carry out social transformations because we were elected to do
> so. But we are doing and will do it within a legal and juridical
> framework. The political Constitution gives us the possibility of
> establishing a new constitution different from the present one,
> and this road we will also use.[1]

In these lines we find the thinking of Salvador Allende. In so
affirming he was deeply convinced that it was possible to advance along
a revolutionary road of structural transformations using the institutionality forged by Chilean capitalist society, attempting to change it
without departure from the rules it laid down. To do that the government had to follow a policy of thoroughgoing changes while at the
same time fulfilling its role as guarantor of public order; to implement
Popular Unity's program on the basis of combining mass activity with
application of prevailing laws presumed to favor such changes. During a
brief period such a project seemed viable: many measures were carried
out which found the bourgeoisie divided and in disarray, and the
headway made by the transformations seemed to justify those in the
popular movement who had long defended this approach. But as we

have seen, immediately after the April national elections the first voices were raised on the Left warning of limitations and obstacles ahead. It had become necessary to reconsider in objectively different circumstances the labor and popular movement's two main tendencies—the Workers' Front strategy of the Socialist Party, and the National Liberation Front strategy of the Communist Party.

The Workers' Front line, adopted by the Socialists in an effort to define class alliances, meant regrouping wage-workers in a front which specifically excluded the bourgeoisie, with the aim of advancing the struggle for the independent demands and goals of the proletariat and its allies. At the Chillán and Linares congresses the Socialists had made this strategy even clearer by defining the socialist character of the process and postulating revolutionary violence as the road to achieving it. During the specific phase of Chilean history that began in 1970, this line brought the Socialists to the following positions:

> The Socialist Party sees the revolutionary process as an uninter-rupted march, with neither stages nor premature consolidations within the existing capitalist system, toward full conquest of power by the workers, aiming simultaneously at fulfillment of still unrealized democratic tasks and of new socialist tasks. Thus the process has a socialist character from the outset. . . . Consid-ered in isolation as a goal in themselves, reforms are no more than reformism. Nationalization of copper and banks and the agrarian reform, important as they are, would not be revolutionary meas-ures if that were their exclusive aim. These reforms become revolutionary when inserted into an overall revolutionary strategy pointing toward replacement of one class by another in manage-ment and control of the new society.

Adding emphasis to this analysis, the Socialists thus appraised the government: "The Popular Unity government will have revolutionary content to the extent that it stops leaning exclusively on bourgeois institutionality and helps open the road to a new institutionality."[2]

The Socialist position was put still more forcefully by the Movement of the Revolutionary Left (MIR) which, being outside of Popular Unity, had no responsibility for the government's tactics. Said MIR general secretary Miguel Enríquez, as quoted in *El Mercurio* of Novem-ber 1, 1971:

The Popular Unity government has dealt a blow to the interests of the ruling class. But by not bringing the masses into the processes and not striking at the state apparatus and institutions, it has become increasingly weak. Despite its positive measures and the progress it has made, the weaknesses and concessions, the temptation in some of its sectors to assume the role of arbiters of the class struggle, leave the workers no alternative but to withdraw some of the confidence they had placed in [the government] and, while supporting its positive measures and opposing its concessions, to define, themselves, the road they must take.

Both positions had a common denominator in the need to win full power for the workers and in deep mistrust of bourgeois institutions, partly government-controlled though these were at the time. But there was a difference of emphasis in that the Socialist position seemed to place high value on the tool that possession of the government represented as leverage for development of new power relations, whereas the MIR proposed an alternative power based exclusively on the energy and capacities of the mobilized masses.

The Communist Party had for many years stated the necessity of uniting all forces tending to favor a basically anti-imperialist and anti-feudal revolution, and saw the "national bourgeoisie"—whose interests such a revolution would supposedly serve—as having a valid place in the National Liberation Front. As Luis Corvalán told the Fourteenth Communist Party Congress in November 1969:

The goal of Popular Unity is to take power and make the revolution. For us Marxists the content of the new power and the character of this revolution are above all determined by reality. We cannot make subjective decisions based on artificial schemes, on pain of slowing the march of the process. This content, this character, are defined by the kind of fundamental contradictions inherent in our society, by the concrete significance of revolutionary changes on our agenda, by the interests that all classes committed to the transformation of society have in common, and finally by the international framework in which the Chilean revolution takes place. That is why the popular power we want to establish and the revolution we need are essentially and objectively anti-imperialist and anti-oligarchy, and lead to socialism.

And, let us say in passing, that is also why certain positions tending to give an immediate socialist character to the process we must set in motion do not strike us as very serious or scientifically rigorous.[3]

Such were the basic positions on the Left which in varying degrees influenced the government leadership and mobilization of the masses in the Chilean process. After the first implementations of the Popular Unity program, it was the pace of the process around which differences were expressed and, as we have seen, in April the Socialists proposed a plebiscite which never took place due to the Communists' opposition.

Then began a period when the chief actors waited offstage. Discipline, more discipline, always discipline was demanded of Chilean workers; and immediately after the April 1971 elections and the level of consciousness it showed, they indicated readiness to support the government's initiative. The government had to carry out the program and, in changing structures, it had to weigh every step; at that stage, all its legitimacy rested on bourgeois institutions, and legitimacy was the justification of each move. In those conditions popular support was secondary: the government's concern was not to develop such support but on the contrary to keep it within legal bounds. The contradictions and limitations this implied were to emerge in the course of the process. The Chilean bourgeoisie, for its part, was expectantly eyeing its two main political spokesmen in hopes of a unified orientation which did not materialize: Christian Democracy was then accepting certain changes just so long as they were made with "respect for democracy," carefully differentiating itself from the National Party which loomed as a retrograde force defending the interests of a few. Yet behind the public statements was the basic fact of two different policies with much in common: to prevent socialist transformations.

In June 1971 something happened that had absolutely nothing to do with the government and the popular movement: a small organization probably infiltrated by the CIA assassinated the Frei government's former interior minister, industrialist Pérez Zujovic. For some days the air was filled with tension, essentially due to the violent attacks launched by Frei and the Christian Democratic sector that sought an alliance with the National Party, charging the government with responsibility for the assassination. The response was lamentably defensive, denying any connection with the affair and repudiating the pseudo-revolutionary group's action, but not seizing the opportunity to denounce the traditional violence of the bourgeoisie and its institutions. The fact that the government had become part of that institutionality imposed its own rules. It remained to be seen whether that institutionality would allow the government to advance a revolutionary policy or whether, on the contrary, it would become an obstacle to the organization and consciousness of the masses.

Until then the Christian Democrats had not succeeded in working out a coherent line vis-à-vis the government. While the Frei administration had had its contradictions with certain well-defined strata of the agrarian and financial bourgeoisie, its essential function had been to develop a modernized version of capitalism. Yet within it there were developmentalist tendencies, mildly nationalistic, toward an expanding economy in which a substantial state sector would favor growth of the industrial bourgeoisie—a policy also responding to pressures by the popular strata among its "clientele." The problem was that those Christian Democratic sectors carried very little weight against the bourgeois class as a whole. We have seen how U.S. imperialism had turned the owners of Chile's most basic industries into junior partners tied to U.S. interests, and the same was true in finance and commerce. At the same time, it was the middle bourgeoisie's weakness relative to the rest of its class that provided a key obstacle to implementing both the Communist Party's national liberation project and the program of Christian Democracy's "progressive" wing.

Disoriented though they were, these strata were strong enough in June 1971 to prevent the bourgeoisie from uniting for the time being. But in July, elections for a deputy in Valparaíso Province produced the first of a series of significant events: the opposition united in putting up a single candidate who defeated Popular Unity by a small margin. Christian Democracy's progressive sectors were unable to halt this trend toward right-wing unification, and in August some parliamentarians and leaders of that tendency left the party to form the Christian Left. Subsequent events would expose Christian Democracy's deeply reactionary essence and, although the schism had qualitative value, it affected neither the party's capacity to win votes and mobilize masses nor its influence in the political and institutional superstructure. On the contrary, once free of its "progressives," the party's leadership could reinforce its positions with the bourgeois opposition and lay claim to be the main alternative to Popular Unity.

In October a bill to delimit the three sectors of the economy was presented in the Senate. Written by Christian Democratic senators Hamilton and Renán Fuentealba, it said:

> Hereby are declared null and void the acts or agreements performed or executed by the state, or agencies or entities comprising or controlled by it or dependent on it, as from October 14, 1971, to acquire stocks or rights of juridically private persons with the purpose of nationalization or state takeover of enterprises producing goods and services, which shall not have been expressly authorized by law in conformity with the provisions of Article 44, No. 16, of the Political Constitution of the State.[4]

The veils concealing the various classes' material interests were beginning to be torn away: Christian Democracy showed its true colors as defender of the propertied bourgeoisie, and humiliated the government under the yoke of the law the latter vowed almost daily to respect. In future, if the bill became law, enterprises that belonged in the Social Production Sector could be brought into it only if the majority of senators and deputies approved—in effect, at the exclusive will and pleasure of Christian Democracy. The government denied the constitutionality of this resolution and a power conflict resulted that was never resolved. The law, the Constitution, and institutionality were becoming increasingly fluid and difficult to define as each class strove assiduously to interpret them in its own way; their other-worldly purity showed itself to be more and more this-worldly and tied to concrete material interests.

Hitherto, government advances along the "institutional road" were based chiefly on two factors. On the one hand, the executive's great freedom of action in a regime which the 1925 Constitution proclaimed to be "presidentialist," thanks to which measures deeply affecting Chile's traditional economic and social structure had been taken. On the other, the alliance with the "middle classes" whose interests on all levels had to be respected. But after the April 1971 elections, which showed the small and still diminishing influence of the Radical Party, the government began to identify Christian Democracy as the political voice of the "middle classes." In consequence, the second determinant of government action hinged increasingly on relations with that party. It is fairly obvious that within this framework mobilization of the masses was limited to serving as leverage in elections, in big popular demonstrations, and in the occupation of enterprises which the program had earmarked for the social sector and which the government's technicians had decided to nationalize. But it was far from easy to confine the masses to the role of guests on these occasions. In the countryside, farmworkers and sharecroppers mobilized with increasing energy and determination, and in August landowners' organizations were complaining that in three provinces alone, 19,000 campesinos were on strike against 761 *fundos,* or large farms. Urban workers seemed to trail behind: their strikes were more specifically economistic, and only on government initiative did they act for longer-term demands. But beneath the surface the various wage-earning strata were undergoing a daily and molecular process of intense, active politicization: the problems of society were no longer the sole concern of more enlightened workers, membership and participation in unions kept increasing, and so did the active membership and public role of the Left parties. Within a few months tens of thousands of men, women, and young people, all of them workers, joined the ranks of the Socialists, Communists, MIR, and MAPU. Tens of thousands of workers in section committees of intervened and state enterprises scrutinized their enterprise leadership, and the more conscious elements began to discuss political power and how to win it. Toward the end of 1971 the government, despite its limitations, was backed by the immense majority of Chilean workers, and the phrase "Este será un gobierno de mierda, pero es mi gobierno"—"This government may be shit but it's mine"—became common currency.

In December 1971, when the forces of bourgeois reaction were in process of consolidating, the opposite was occurring in popular ranks. Whereas partisans of the "politico-institutional road" still could not get their act together, and the gap widened between them and the middle bourgeoisie and Christian Democracy, the theoretical and tactical positions of partisans of the nascent revolutionary Left showed increasing signs of maturity.

A series of events in December highlighted from different angles the cumulative struggles that were sharpening day by day. For the first time since the April elections the bourgeoisie tried an unusual experiment: obscure organizations, behind which lurked the National Party and the ultrarightist Patria y Libertad movement, organized a women's protest march against "shortages and the high cost of living," to which Christian Democracy gave tacit approval. The demonstration through Santiago's streets became tumultuous since young Patria y Libertad activists, always available for any kind of excesses, accompanied and "protected" the women. There were spontaneous counterdemonstrations by Popular Unity supporters, and police repressed the resulting confrontation by their usual methods. Within less than twenty-four hours the Christian Democrats decided to bring constitutional charges against Interior Minister José Tohá, aiming to remove him from office as responsible for the "aggression against thousands of women." Next day the National Party associated itself with the charges. The "Tohá case" resulted in something of a draw: the reactionary majority in Congress got the interior minister fired, but President Allende, while accepting the legality of this measure, appointed Tohá to another important ministry.

The legality that the government had decided to respect was in fact proving daily more favorable to reaction and unfavorable for the revolutionary process. And during the whole period up to October 1972, it was precisely on this terrain of legality that the bourgeoisie tried to paralyze implementation of the Popular Unity program and to impede mobilization of the masses: by means of the Constitution and the powers of Congress, the courts, and the office of the comptroller.

In the same month President Allende told the Sixth CUT Congress:

Everyone knows that the Chilean process presents more difficulties because we have pursued it here within the contours of bourgeois democracy and within the laws of bourgeois democracy; within our Constitution, which is not of our making. We are going to modify the Constitution and enact the laws of the revolutionary government. . . . We know that elsewhere there was no alternative to fighting with arms in hand, and we respect and admire the heroism of peoples who followed that course. Our case is different but our revolution is nonetheless an authentic one. And as has been said here by the president of CUT, compañero and friend Luis Figueroa, this revolution has a minimal social cost. Let those who today resort to violence listen and understand. This Chilean revolution has a minimal social cost.[5]

The problem was not resolved, and the use of legality and bourgeois-democratic institutions to implement a revolutionary process awakened mistrust in a sector of the Left that feared demobilization of the masses and the castration of socialist strategy. A document that became known as the "Linares Manifesto," signed by Popular Unity and the MIR of Linares Province, as well as the Campesino Communal Council of Linares, was published on December 19. Subsequently the Linares leadership of the Communist Party was repudiated. Essentially the document was a call for campesino councils, that is, for agricultural workers to join in actions independent of the initiatives of government agencies. It called for the intensification of agrarian reform, including such measures as immediate expropriation of all *fundos* over eighty hectares without reserving to landowners any rights in land, buildings, machinery, or animals, and for lowering the limit not affected to forty hectares. It was a program reflecting the heightened activity of poor campesinos, the limitations imposed by existing agrarian-reform laws, and the potential of a Left revolutionary tendency in the popular movement. But the Socialist Party and other Popular Unity organizations did not take it up on a national scale, and the Communist Party openly attacked it as contrary to the alliance with the "middle classes" that had to be secured in the countryside. The owners of farms over forty hectares, and especially those over eighty hectares, were in fact generally capitalists; they figured in the Chilean social scale as the agricultural middle-entrepreneur sector who, having invested previous surpluses in those properties, stood in direct line of succession from the agrarian oligarchy most starkly antagonistic to the poor peasantry.

Developments in the first quarter of 1972 took place basically within the above framework of continuous opposition skirmishes against presidential initiatives, seeking parliamentary obstruction of more and more elemental administrative measures and finally denying the government funds for the school program, among others. The use and abuse of all institutional mechanisms to hamper the development of the Social Production Sector were the role of the comptroller's office and of the Supreme Court. The comptroller invariably vetoed all industrial intervention decrees, rejecting the legal arguments of the ministry of the economy. The courts turned the officials named to administer such industries into defendants, and suspended provincial authorities appointed by the executive.

At the El Arrayán meeting in February no alternative was defined precisely and, as far as developing the economic plan and the class-alliance policy was concerned, the meeting set the pattern of waiting it out. In March there were new efforts at requisitioning enterprises that were among the original ninety-one earmarked for the social sector. This provoked violent attacks in Congress, more rejections by the comptroller's office, cries of illegality from the employer group SOFOFA (Sociedad de Fomento Fabril—Association of Manufacturers), and finally Christian Democrat charges of "contempt of Congress."

And now the direct representatives of bourgeois entrepreneur groups and of the petty bourgeoisie, who had been accustomed to intervene only in defense of their immediate "guild" interests, began to take on strength. Troubled by the seeming indecisiveness of intermediary political leaderships, they to an extent displaced them in the political arena and certainly as challengers of the popular government. In March the Production and Trade Confederation, comprising nearly all Chilean property owners of every level and sector, proclaimed that in the countryside "the simple law of the jungle prevails and the situation seems out of control," in industry "we are confronted by *faits accomplis* as in the cases of Ceresita and Sindelen, due to the forced march to incorporate industry in the state sector," and in trade there was "an acute shortage of various commodities"; in sum, ". . . we don't want to seem like prophets of doom, but after all the economy is ruled by laws. Certain actions produce certain effects."[6]

Meanwhile conflicts in every area of Chilean society steadily increased. Strikes in industry, confrontations in the countryside, demonstrations by *pobladores* and students, pressures by the different economic groups—all combined to harden conflicting union, employer, and political interests and to make relations between the different state powers less and less flexible.

In April the government tried again to reach an understanding with Christian Democracy—and let us note that on this as on subsequent occasions the initiative came from the former. Not only did these talks fail to produce the anticipated result, but they also led to the departure from Popular Unity of a Radical Party splinter, which declared: "If the plan proposed for the three areas were approved, small and middle producers would continue in a state of total uncertainty and insecurity." Actually the Christian Democrats, in covert alliance with

Popular Unity's bourgeois sectors, had failed in their efforts to bring the government to its knees in order to reduce its content to a populist-type program and to limit its authority in such a way as to guarantee capitalist development in Chile. Political relations were then fluid enough to maintain some points of contact between a Christian Democratic fraction and a sector of Popular Unity and of the government, but these coincidences never jelled into a coherent position. At the same time, the popular movement was becoming more radicalized, making it clear that a compromise in implementing the program would produce a deep split in the working class and lead to new and different confrontations.

Right after the failure of the "dialogue" with Christian Democracy, both Popular Unity and the opposition organized "monster marches," which brought out hundreds of thousands of people in each case but of very different social composition. On each side of the dividing line the classes stood out in even bolder relief.

By May the development plans revealed marked weaknesses. Chile was approaching a crossroads, and the institutional system that had given it forty years of civilian government was ceasing to function in the face of sharpened class struggle between workers pushing for a new society and a resisting bourgeoisie. It was a month of countless pronunciamentos on every battlefront, noticeably reactionary and anti-government, by the courts and the comptroller's office. Far from favoring the revolutionary process, institutionality had become more and more a powerful obstacle.

The results of the CUT elections in May were unexpected for the Left: Communists, Socialists, and Christian Democrats were elected in that order but with small margins, each with about 30 percent of the vote. Organized labor's support for Christian Democracy proved to be far from negligible.

The leadership of the popular movement faced two divergent roads, and the two lines within Popular Unity called for definition. The Lo Curro meeting ended early in June.

Political parties represent social classes, but that representation is neither homogeneous nor direct. In the first place, social classes are made up of different groupings: the whole class shares a central nucleus of definition and historical perspective, but objectives within it do not always coincide, especially with regard to short-term situations. Representation is not direct because short- and long-term interests come clothed in ideological vestments, differences of habit, tradition, language, and aspiration. Finally, parties generate an ideology that takes on its own dynamic, not becoming independent of class but impeding a direct and clear relationship.

In a process of big transformations and massive participation by all sectors of society, political parties lose their neat distinctness, top leaderships are exposed to strong and varying influences, and there is intercommunication between different parties, which converge or diverge according to the period and intensity of the class struggle. This took place in Chile, some converging and some diverging, inside and outside Popular Unity. When in mid-1972 the "politico-institutional road" showed signs of exhaustion, the distance widened between left parties which conceived the process differently.

> We Communists believe we have duties to fulfill toward our people, our working class, the government; that is why we are ready and determined to overcome this crisis, holding high the banner of unity of the workers, unity of the people—of applying the Popular Unity program without modification or illegality. Some say that legality and institutions are an insurmountable obstacle and fetter preventing our advance. For our part we are convinced that prevailing institutions and legality are not particularly helpful to us. They are certainly a brake, an obstacle to development of the revolutionary process, but they are not an insurmountable obstacle since it has been shown up to now that important things can be done within this legal framework, and that what can be achieved depends not so much on the law as on the struggle, on organization, on mobilization of the masses, on the relationship of forces at a given moment. Moreover, we don't believe that any possibility exists at the moment of modifying this legality, these institutions, by any means, whether they be legal or extralegal.[7]

The difference between this and the Socialist position was much more than one of shading:

> The bourgeoisie preach holy respect of legality when legality serves to reinforce the capitalist system or, as is now the case in Chile, when they use it to brake the [revolutionary] process. But no sooner does it become an obstacle to their political objectives

—as from another angle is also happening here today—than they put legality in their pockets, consign it to the wastebasket, and rush into illegal and subversive actions and coups d'état. If the bourgeoisie themselves abandon legality when it suits them, there can be no reason for a revolutionary to fear and respect it. The Socialist Party's Twenty-Third Congress pointed out that the particular conditions in which Popular Unity took government office should not be a pretext for the government to play arbiter in the class struggle. It also maintained that the workers' presence in the government cannot mean dependence of the mass movement on the government apparatus.[8]

This stance of rejecting bourgeois legality, and of the need to destroy and overcome it by mass consciousness, organization, and mobilization, was taken with equal force by MAPU and the Christian Left inside Popular Unity and by MIR outside it. But the correlation of forces at the top of Popular Unity and particularly in the government headed by Allende, favored the Communist theses. At bottom the Communist position rested on the need for understandings with sectors that held fast to the state structure, that had a populist base and a middle-entrepreneur social leadership. That is, the line implied re-affirmation of legality in the sense of the bourgeois state super-structure, and maintenance of and guarantees to the interests of the middle bourgeoisie. In a word, it meant development of Chilean capitalist structures in a new, advanced phase of reformism.

> Chile has given itself a popular government corresponding to an advanced democracy that assures favorable conditions for the struggle for socialism. For the working class to fulfill its revolutionary role in this advanced democracy and with this popular government, it is absolutely necessary to have a very clearly defined mobilizing policy of alliances with the urban and rural masses and with the small and middle bourgeoisie, so that imperialism, the landlords, and the financial oligarchy may be isolated.[9]

This Communist Party line was approved by the assembled leadership of Popular Unity and its content was immediately reaffirmed on the economic level: Social Production Sector enterprises had to be profitable and produce surpluses, inflation was to be reduced by limited wage and salary adjustments, and tax policy left unchanged. On the social level, the alliance with the "middle classes" was reaffirmed, with strong censure of any mobilizations for nationalization of enterprises and large landholdings not included in the Popular Unity program. On the political level, this economic and social policy was to be implemented by an agreement with representatives of the sectors to which it was addressed, that is, with Christian Democracy.

The talks began immediately after Lo Curro, and on June 17 Christian Democracy's president, Renán Fuentealba, said:

> There are left- and right-wing sectors that want a confrontation. This helps no one. Our party has acted within its political ethic and is defending its ideas with all its strength. The president of the Republic invited us for talks about a Christian Democratic policy proposal. We will not change our position. We remain and will remain in the opposition, and will accordingly denounce and condemn any action in which the government departs from its commitments and from institutional guarantees and which leads to a nationalization process that will only culminate in dictatorship.[10]

This language revealed the internal weakness of Christian Democracy's "progressive" sector relative to the sector representing the interests of Frei and the big industrial bourgeoisie. Fuentealba, taking his seat at the discussion table with the obligation to answer to the most reactionary sectors pressuring him from inside his party, accordingly and in advance hardened his line toward the government. A few days later came this declaration from nearly all of Christian Democracy's senators: "We senators declare that the proposals made by the government will be analyzed with utmost care, and the positions taken by Christian Democracy on constitutional reform will be resolutely defended."[11]

Despite the efforts of the government and a sector of Popular Unity, the talks broke down at the end of that month; no agreement was reached, although the Christian Democratic sector then controlling most of the party's guiding organs was committed to reaching one. We must then ask why, in such opportune conditions, the agreement that both parties apparently wanted was not made.

In the first place, any economic development project must obtain the necessary funds for broad, dynamic, and stable growth. At that time in Chile such investments could only be had from two sources: expropriation of the bourgeoisie, or greater exploitation of the workers.

Hence the alliance as projected lacked stability, and the interests of society's most basic classes—big bourgeoisie and proletariat—would have clashed in short order, since the projected alliance did not resolve that contradiction. Furthermore, the middle bourgeoisie shared, with only trifling differences, the big bourgeoisie's ideological models, so that it naturally tended to take the ruling sector's side in periods of sharpened class struggle. In conclusion, we must also note that the class struggle no longer permitted an unstable equilibrium such as the plan called for, since the working class's consciousness and organization, too highly developed to be straitjacketed by bourgeois institutionality, were bursting all the seams of the legal order. Hence the middle bourgeoisie contemplated with deep mistrust any long-term understanding with the workers.

The sector of Popular Unity that insisted on moving ahead with new forms of mobilization had its reply to the policy of dialogue and frustrated agreement with Christian Democracy. In July the People's Assembly met in the city of Concepción. It consisted of Socialists, Radicals, Mapucistas, Christian Leftists, and Miristas responding to a call from the Socialist Regional Committee in Concepción. These people met to seek out new organic and agitational forms that would rescue the popular movement from the bog of vain efforts for superstructural agreements, and to criticize the limitless submission of government and Popular Unity leadership to bourgeois-democratic legality. Despite the success of this gathering, which brought together broad and combative sectors of Concepción workers and *pobladores,* it went no further. In face of indignant cries from the Right and from Congress, the regional leaders of the Popular Unity parties—in particular those of the Socialist Party—were repudiated by their respective central committees and by President Allende.

When the Popular Unity-Christian Democracy talks dragged to a halt in August, the employers' associations began to raise their heads in earnest and take the initiative in many situations. On the twenty-first a national business stoppage was called in "energetic protest against the government's unfortunate economic policy which has had grave consequences for all sectors of the country, especially for our associations, which have suffered heavy decapitalization due to growing inflation and general scarcity of goods."[12]

A strike of Christian Democratic-oriented high school students on

September 1 provoked counterdemonstrations and a real pitched battle in Santiago's streets, with hundreds of casualties. Popular Unity's reply to the mass mobilizations by reactionary forces was a call to celebrate the second anniversary of the victory of September 4, 1970, which brought out the biggest political demonstration in Chilean history. About a million people paraded through Santiago in support of Allende's government.

By then the cumulative inflation for the first eight months of 1972 had reached 63.5 percent, and by September 30 it would be 99.8 percent. This was due not only to the blind forces of the economy but also to a hoarding and speculation in all sectors and on every level of Chilean society that completely prevented the normal capitalist mechanisms from imposing traditional models of distribution.

In that period a crude conspiratorial effort by Alfredo Canales, an openly reactionary and authoritarian general, was aborted. It got no support from the bourgeoisie or from imperialism, already then busy preparing a full-dress confrontation with the popular movement.

Meanwhile the employers' associations moved downstage, and plans went ahead for the first bourgeois insurrection to recapture economic, social, and political control. Open confrontation between the real protagonists in the class struggle, proletariat and bourgeoisie, was approaching.

To face that situation the workers needed to gain more power and more control of the economic apparatus, to strengthen the popular movement not only quantitatively but also qualitatively, to improve and surpass traditional sociopolitical organizations, and to create new forms of action and agitation. But recent experience suggested that the institutional program's limitations had weakened the popular movement's mobilizing capacity and confidence in its own forces, and it surrendered its initiative—in a disciplined way, as requested—to the top leadership in the government, political parties, and trade unions.

A moment was coming which would test to the utmost the sinews of all social forces, and which would not find the workers in the best condition to meet the test. Far from that, it was the employers' associations representing the various bourgeois groups who were clearly taking the offensive.

The "politico-institutional road" was revealing its limitations and the disadvantageous contradictions which, even in Chile's unusually democratic conditions, arose from respect for and submission to capitalist state legality.

1. *El Mercurio* (Santiago de Chile), March 7, 1971.
2. Carlos Altamirano, *Decisión Revolucionaria* (Santiago de Chile: Quimantú, 1973).
3. Luis Corvalán, *Chili, les Communistes dans la Marche au Socialisme* (Paris: Editions Sociales, 1972).
4. *El Mercurio,* October 15, 1971.
5. *El Mercurio,* December 8, 1971.
6. Jorge Fontaine, in *El Mercurio,* March 14, 1972. Ceresita is a paint company and Sindelen a manufacturer of electric meters, owned by Mitsubishi.
7. Luis Corvalán, chairman of the Chilean Communist Party, at a press conference, May 25, 1972.
8. Carlos Altamirano, *Decisión Revolucionaria* (Santiago de Chile: Quimantú, 1973).
9. Orlando Millas, in the Communist daily *El Siglo* (Santiago de Chile), June 5, 1972.
10. Renán Fuentealba, in *El Mercurio,* June 17, 1972.
11. *El Mercurio,* June 20, 1972.
12. *El Mercurio,* August 21, 1972.

5 OCTOBER 1972: THE FIRST BOURGEOIS INSURRECTION

In the period between April 1971 and October 1972 we have noted an unstable equilibrium of forces whose chief components were the popular government and Christian Democracy. Throughout that stage the government relied essentially on the legitimacy of its origins and the legality of its actions to take fragments of economic power from imperialism and the big Chilean bourgeoisie. At first disoriented, these later succeeded in substantially regrouping their forces, uniting their different sectors against the threat to their traditional domination and, by use of mechanisms constitutionally vested in Congress and the courts and the comptroller's office, putting an effective brake on the process. The government slowed its advance, repeatedly sought a basis of agreement with the middle bourgeoisie through "dialogue" with Christian Democracy, and consequently made only occasional and partial use of the enormous potential of revolutionary support by the Chilean masses. Meanwhile the class struggle in city and countryside came more and more to the boil in the absence of the traditional use of state repressive mechanisms.

By the end of September 1972 the situation had notably changed relative to April 1971. Now it was the government that was on the defensive. The bourgeoisie had considerably strengthened its unity, its capacity to mobilize masses of people, its use of prevailing institutionality, its control of a great part of the mass media. At the same time there was a downward plunge in the economy, inflation was reaching the runaway stage, and big capitalist groups substantially controlling distribution were using their capital for speculation so that hoarding and basic consumer shortages were a daily provocation to the workers.

In that situation the bourgeoisie, having failed to turn the Allende administration into a new reformist-populist government, believed the moment ripe for decisive confrontation by exerting the full weight of their economic power, the institutions they controlled, and their political representation. A combined offensive by all of these could, they thought, create chaos and tear Chilean society apart. They hoped to oblige the armed forces to overthrow the government, or at least to make the government waver on all the positions it had hitherto maintained. Tendencies were developing within the opposition that favored a possible coup, since Christian Democracy had moved from indecisiveness and demagogy to an implacably reactionary stance against presidential initiatives. The government's offers and the Communist Party's guarantees had not sufficed to clinch a policy of alliance and understanding.

After the collapse of the June talks which showed that a centrist and reformist line was not viable in Chile, the middle bourgeoisie's leading sectors lined up openly behind the big bourgeoisie and their objectives, and this helped to close the ranks of Christian Democratic leadership around the policies of Eduardo Frei. At the same time, late in August, when the employer insurrection was being hatched, it was Christian Democratic senator Fuentealba who warned the government in essence that it could not use the *carabineros* and armed forces to repress rightist demonstrations by students and businessmen—groups that were becoming daily more violent and provocative. Thus Christian Democracy not only aimed to neutralize the government in the intensifying class struggle, but publicly and openly appealed to the armed forces for support for its plan of action. This was no accident, for top officers were under growing pressure at the time to provoke internal demonstrations against the government. The Christian Democrats, as their nonsupport of General Canales showed, certainly intended no coup at that moment; but they were preparing the ground to prevent the government from using army and police—as it was legally empowered to do—on the eve of the insurrectionary employers' stoppage in October. In that way Christian Democracy through its "progressive" leadership gave a helping hand to the bourgeoisie's projected attack on the proletariat, while waiting to spell out in the course of events what attitude it would take toward a military putsch.

Since the Lo Curro agreements were proving not only elusive but unworkable—for the more that concessions were made to the "middle classes," the more Christian Democracy's position hardened—Popular Unity was on the defensive, trailing behind the government. And the government was left without any policy to pursue: it could only keep marking time until new factors might let it regain the initiative. As for the working masses, they were looked upon as nothing more than reference points, very useful for holding big demonstrations and celebrating anniversaries but under a discipline reminiscent of a corral—a school of submission to the paternal decisions of top Popular Unity and government figures. In a revolutionary process nothing is more vital than the participation on all fronts and at all times of those masses who, from being passive objects controlled by the ruling classes and economic forces, become decisive subjects in the material and social world around them. Up to the last days of September 1972 Chilean workers had remained in the rearguard, as a combat force with all muscles tensed but held in reserve. They had learned that the bosses—*los momios,* or the "mummies"—could be licked; they were participating in the management of state enterprises in the Social Production Sector; in the countryside they were mobilizing ever more effectively to defeat the landowners; and above all they were massively swelling the Left parties' ranks. But the straitjacket that had been put on the Chilean process by those who led it down the narrow lane of bourgeois-democratic legality, of an institutionality that more and more obviously did not favor it in the bitter class struggle, was heavy and darkly ominous ballast. The employers, when the time came for their insurrection, were in optimum condition for it, facing a weakened government, a Popular Unity off-balance and passive, and large numbers of workers who did not realize their potential strength and had not developed their own initiative.

The reactionary forces began their concerted action in the first week of October.

On October 4 the highest court in France embargoed a $1,360,000 Chilean copper shipment due at Le Havre, in a lawsuit brought by the U.S.'s Kennecott Corporation, ex-owner of El Teniente, the world's largest subterranean mine, located in Chile and nationalized on July 4, 1971. By putting Chile's exports under threat of expropriation in any capitalist country, imperialism showed how far and wide it could extend its tentacles.

On October 7 representatives of the parties in the Democratic Federation (Christian Democratic, National, Radical Democratic, and Radical Left), newly set up to consolidate antigovernment action by all reactionary forces, launched an offensive marked by various shadings within their common purpose. National Party senator Francisco Bulnes proclaimed: "An originally legitimate government that systematically and deliberately violates the Constitution becomes an illegitimate government; in the National Party's view this government has become illegitimate."[1] Senator Bulnes, known as "Marquis Bulnes" for his ludicrous aristocratic pretensions, represented the interests of Chile's smoldering oligarchy. On the same day Radical Democratic senator Julio Durán, choleric defender of central and southern Chile's middle and big landlords, said: "Allende has deviated from our political Constitution." Christian Democratic senator Patricio Aylwin charged the president with staging "a democratic farce" and violating the Statute of Guarantees established before November 4, 1970.

On October 9 the "employer guilds"—that is, the various associations of property owners—went into action. León Vilarín, an obscure character who had made two U.S. trips during the year and who presided over the Truck Owners Confederation, called an indefinite stoppage with the flimsy pretext of protesting against "the conflict imposed on transport in the province of Aisén." It was a challenge not to be taken lightly. This confederation embraced 169 "unions" of truck owners all across the land, in effect totally controlling highway transport. More than half of the country's fuel, raw materials, ocean cargoes, and foodstuffs was transported by road. Confederation members ranged from owners of thirty or more heavy modern trucks to the modest possessor of one broken-down vehicle with over ten years on the road. Vilarín had managed to buy up nearly everyone in the business, thanks to generous dollar donations from the CIA, as a U.S. senate investigating committee would later show.

On October 10 the Democratic Confederation brought out over 100,000 Santiagans for a demonstration in which a National Party orator declared: "We want no more declarations. Enough of complaints and diagnoses. We have had too many words. The hour for action has struck." [2]

On October 13 the hour struck for most of the entrepreneurial groups controlled by reaction: "The Retail Trade and Small Industry Confederation, Taxi Drivers Union, Production and Trade Confederation, and National Confederation of Small Industry and Artisans declare from today a national stoppage in support of the truckers' association." [3]

The fuse was lit. The ordeal by fire had begun. On the same day the Association of Manufacturers (SOFOFA), representing middle and big industry—that is, its proprietors—agreed to "instruct industrialists to halt their activities indefinitely as from today."

It is important to note the success of the big bourgeoisie, especially those belonging to SOFOFA, in obtaining the backing and active support of the middle and small property-owning bourgeoisie. It was in the abovementioned organizations that small businessmen and industrialists were in effect concentrated, while middle and big businessmen belonged to the Production and Trade Confederation along with the middle and big industrialists who ran it.

Next day the opposition parties unanimously backed the employer guilds' strike movement, instructing their members and leaders to participate fully in the reactionary offensive. Students at the Catholic University also joined the stoppage, and the medical profession declared itself in "permanent session" to "observe the course of events."

On October 15 this editorial appeared in the Chilean big bourgeoisie's newspaper *El Mercurio,* proud dean of the Latin American press and financed at the time by the CIA: "If legality is being used to pull Chile off its constitutional foundations and gradually implant the dictatorship of the proletariat, we would have the paradox of the present defenders of public order taking the side of Marxist revolution —that is, against the prevailing order by definition—while those who disobey that revolutionary authority would be on the side of public order and constitutional guarantees." At that moment the various tendencies of the bourgeoisie all pointed in one direction—to stop the process of change once and for all and assure lasting protection of their interests; but shadings still persisted. Thus *El Mercurio* suggested:

Hadn't the time come to bring in the armed forces and depose Allende by force? Actually the call to the "present defenders of public order" could not have been clearer, and the essence of the *Mercurio* line was a "juridical" reply to partisans of the "politico-institutional road." For since Marxists were "by definition" against the prevailing order, legality was on the side of those who opposed the Marxist government, and the armed forces could not let themselves be used to prevent its overthrow.

The country had divided into two great blocs that seemed to have no other point of contact except confrontations. The ubiquitous class struggle had polarized all active elements in Chilean society, and there seemed to be no corner left for the undecided or neutral. Yet there were such elements, important at that moment and later fundamental as the battle intensified: the armed forces.

In responding to the truck owners' stoppage the government was fully aware that the strike was a decisive test of its whole policy by the bourgeoisie, not merely a trade-association matter. And to confront the challenge it chose from all weapons available the one it had used up until then: legal mechanisms vested in the executive to control an important part of public administration. Also, so far as the ambiguities of the situation allowed, it made use of the armed forces' constitutional subordination to the president of the Republic. Thus the interior ministry declared a state of emergency in thirteen provinces, including Santiago, placing them under military authority.

In the armed forces at that time there was no cohesion around a single position. Nor had there been in October 1970 when Generals René Schneider and Carlos Prats, representing one position, prevented a coup d'état in which other generals were involved. This had meant a weakening of the putschist sector, a weakening which Allende had skillfully nurtured, always within the bounds of legality and with studious respect for the armed forces' traditions, their promotion and retirement mechanisms, and their economic and social privileges. By also assigning many officers to managerial positions in state enterprises and appointing one as minister of mining in April 1972, he had kept the armed forces as a whole dissociated from the transformation/confrontation process that the country was undergoing. They were not distant enough from it, however, to keep the views and definitions of the officer corps from burgeoning, influenced more and more by the rightist parties and especially by the fascistic Patria y Libertad movement; but despite this Allende could at that point still count on their not being able to act on the side of reaction without occasioning a deep split in their ranks which would have plunged the country into civil war. The high-ranking officers who acted as heads of provincial governments in October 1972 emerged as arbiters of the situation; their decisions caused pendulum swings in an already unstable balance of forces. And they remained in that role through the whole state-of-emergency period.

From October on, the armed forces' role in Chilean society was considerably strengthened. Without clearly defining it at the time, they asserted themselves as arbiters in government-opposition relationships, and the struggle for their support intensified. In that struggle the "politico-institutional road" thesis revealed its dialectical limitations of tactical strength and strategic weakness, resulting from its strict self-confinement within prevailing constitutional and legal margins of action.

The state of emergency did not prevent the bourgeois insurrection from spreading: on October 18, bus and taxi-bus owners started an indefinite national strike. On the same day strikes were called by bank employees, physicians, lawyers, dentists, merchant marine officers, some high school students, and University of Chile professors, who joined in violent antigovernment demonstrations in most cities throughout Chile.

On October 20 the united reactionary parties declared:

> Sole responsibility for the conditions which gave rise to the conflict . . . that we Chileans are undergoing rests on the government headed by Señor Allende, which has consistently violated its commitments and whose disastrous economic policy has created total chaos. . . . Faithful to their democratic tradition, the confederated parties will fight unswervingly in fulfillment of their duties, even if this leads them to the most extreme consequences.[4]

Also on October 20 the Appeals Court began hearing a suit against a government minister at the instance of the Right, and one of his measures was declared illegal by the comptroller's office.

The opposition parties indeed aimed to arrive at "the most extreme consequences," to wit, removal of the government, or at least its surrender. Yet after almost two weeks of the employer strike they seemed no nearer their goal. What was it that blocked the road?

When employers forming SOFOFA, organ of Chile's industrial entre-preneurs, called on their affiliates to "paralyze their [business] activi-ties for an indefinite period," they unleashed a movement whose consequences for their interests they did not suspect. We have seen that until that time the working class was responding in a disciplined way to government and Popular Unity initiatives. Conflicting economic de-mands had been resolved by traditional methods forged in the class struggle in Chile, and with rare exceptions employers could continue managing and enjoying their private property in nearly all production units. Among small- and middle-industry workers there were larger numbers of both Christian Democratic and MIR elements, due to Popular Unity's lack of a program for that proletarian sector. When the employers tried to implement their trade associations' instructions they met with a united, conscious, and combative response from workers, who decided to keep plants in production without employers or man-agers. Within a few days most of the country's industries were in the hands of their workers: faced with the employer lockout, they showed in practice that the production process did not need bosses. This active response by the proletariat showed that its level of consciousness, maturity, and organization surpassed the practice and orientation of Popular Unity, and represented a barrier far more formidable than legality to reactionary insurrectionism. It was a consciousness and a decisiveness born in the work centers, factories, and social and private sector enterprises, whether big, middle-sized, or small. The workers' actions against the employer stoppage overran all self-imposed limita-tions in respect to the size of enterprises: suddenly the bosses loomed as a single class, a single enemy. Now that virtually all factories were in their workers' hands, all the discussions about how many enterprises should pass into the Social Production Sector appeared ridiculous and sterile. The "politico-institutional road" likewise seemed to be super-seded by the events the bourgeoisie had set in motion, since it was no longer up to Congress and the Executive to determine the country's social relations and economic structures.

In October, then, proletariat and bourgeoisie faced each other with-out intermediaries, as open class enemies, with respect to the concrete problem of production and distribution. At the same time divisions within the working class were immediately erased and transcended: Socialists, Communists, Mapucistas stood shoulder to shoulder with Miristas and even Christian Democrats, all fighting to prevent an employer victory, united in occupation of the industries, with the same concern to obtain raw materials and distribute "their" plants' production. The October days sealed for a moment the most solid and compact working-class unity, above and beyond all previous differences. Certainly the Popular Unity parties were not aloof from this battle and it was their members, especially Socialists, who promoted the great "takeover" of Chile's industries; but everywhere they found a proletariat ready to go even farther. In fact, in the October days worker-created structures arose which were not envisaged in the Constitution nor in Popular Unity's plans and program.

The workers immediately learned that supply problems could be more easily resolved if they coordinated their efforts in sectors embracing a group of factories. Also that it was easier to defend the sector, its buildings and streets, against fascist sabotage gangs if they acted together in a given geographic area. Likewise with collective transportation and other problems. Thus those October days saw the birth of the *cordones industriales* (industrial-area committees), organized on the basis of direct worker representation in the various industrial zones' factory units. At the same time Supply and Price Committees (JAPs), organized mainly by women in urban neighborhoods, concerned themselves with ensuring the availability of essential food supplies, with or without the cooperation of local merchants. The JAPs denounced and requisitioned hoarded commodities, helped reopen closed stores, and made their owners serve the people.

Over much broader areas new group tasks were undertaken by *comandos comunales* (neighborhood committees) which resulted from cooperation between representatives of the *cordones,* unions, JAPs, mothers' centers, neighborhood committees, student centers, *poblador* committees, and Left parties. All of these got together to name a leadership committee that grappled with the most immediate problems: defense and security against sabotage, maintenance of production levels, methods of community mobilization, public order in the *poblaciones,* distribution channels for basic foodstuffs, relations with nearby campesino councils to assure supply of farm products. In fulfillment of all this—which in practice meant local power replacing the whole previous structure—representatives of the various organs comprising the *comandos comunales* distributed tasks, assumed responsibilities, and planned the advance of society according to the situation in each sector.

The workers showed in October 1972 that they not only could run industrial production without employers, but could move the country ahead parallel with the state structures that the bourgeoisie's action seemed to have dislocated. In the streets and factories of Chile's chief cities unity was forged, in action, among workers, *pobladores,* students, housewives, and public and private white-collar workers. They discussed ways of organizing together beyond political party membership, showing their will to bar the road to reaction and keep the country from taking any step backward.

In the October days it was the conscious action of the Chilean masses, led by the urban proletariat, that stood up to the employer insurrection and finally defeated it. In so doing they reached the highest level of class consciousness and organization in Latin American history. They developed a revolutionary perspective which went beyond the Popular Unity program, building a people's unity on a qualitatively higher foundation, bypassing the legality for which the bourgeoisie had shown their contempt.

And this—together with the armed forces' neutrality—was what blocked the program of the employer guilds, which had confidently expected to paralyze the country and provoke chaos by narrowing popular support of the government to a minimum and bringing in the military on their side. It was the workers who defeated this plan, shifted labor and *poblador* sympathies away from Christian Democracy, and achieved a unity and perspective superior to anything in the Chilean process up to that time.

As an example of how the workers extended their action to all the nation's cities, this is what happened in the southern industrial zone of Concepción:

> Workers of the Cerrillos Metallurgical Plant proceeded yesterday to take over installations in the Talcahuano industrial complex, with demands that the enterprise be intervened and transferred into the social sector. Participating in the takeover were 140 of the industry's white- and blue-collar employees who yesterday barred executives and engineers from entering the

plant. The plant produces metal structures, water tanks, and steel beams. According to reports there is at the moment no labor conflict, either economic or social, to justify the takeover, which appears to have been carried out as reprisal by the workers against the enterprise due to the present situation in the country. It was also stated that the Cerrillos Metallurgical Plant was not included among the ninety-one enterprises listed by the government for statification. The plant manager appeared yesterday with lawyer F. Saneger before the First Court of Talcahuano to lodge a complaint about the situation.[5]

We find here the principal factors: the workers' unanimity, their demand for transfer of the enterprise to the Social Production Sector regardless of the fact that it was only a middle-sized plant, their motivation not any specific conflict but in response to the employers' action, and finally the extreme weakness of the employers, who found no recourse other than "lodging a complaint about the situation" in court.

The government had by then gathered considerable strength and the bourgeoisie were frightened: day by day they were losing factories and, with them, economic power; Christian Democratic influence on the worker and *poblador* was waning, and their declared aim of paralyzing the country was getting nowhere. Requisitioning trucks with the help of Left party members, the government got land transport partially moving again, the JAPs were making shopkeepers reopen their doors to meet the people's needs, blue- and white-collar workers were on the job and seeing that goods were distributed and sold. And precisely because of the strength of popular response, the employer strike failed to spark military intervention. Now they had to confront not only the government but a new power in formation, outside of institutionality and hence much more dangerous to their interests. President Allende told the country that the employer strike had cost it around $100 million; a large part of that cost was in unsold perishable goods, so that merchants began to react against the promoters of what was becoming a calamity for their small businesses. The bourgeoisie saw their social strength ebbing daily, and by the end of October nearly all sectors of that class were clamoring to end the strike and seek an understanding with the government.

The insurrection had failed. A new interclass relation of forces had emerged which opened three qualitatively different and divergent alternatives to the government. The first was to develop popular power, with the short-term perspective of completing the destruction of bourgeois institutionality and creating new revolutionary laws. The second was to deepen existing legality on the basis of agreements between the proletariat and other social classes and strata, categorically excluding the middle and big bourgeoisie. The third was to reaffirm the model hitherto followed, of alliance with the "middle classes" and subjection to the established social, juridical, and political system.

Never in Chilean history had the capitalist system and all its institutions been so weak, diminished, and vacillating. Congress, courts, and comptroller's office had teamed up with the employer guilds in an anticonstitutional scheme to overthrow another state authority. That scheme had failed and those institutions stood naked before the country as allies of a defeated minority class. Even more important, embryos of an alternative power had emerged now that the *cordones industriales,* campesino councils, and *comandos comunales* had shown that they could organize vast sectors of the people to administer public affairs and keep the country going outside state structures. However, there was a third player in the game: the armed forces.

Those who lack confidence in the people's energy and their organizing and fighting capacity always produce a final argument to prove the impossibility of making a revolution, of destroying the capitalist state and building a new social order based on working-class leadership: the techniques, organization, and firepower of modern repressive apparatuses. Essentially this is no more than a repetition of the German Social Democratic reformists' arguments at the end of the last century, in spite of which various revolutions have succeeded since then. As a clincher they bring in the question of "global context" and the military power of imperialism, forgetting the defeat imperialism suffered in Vietnam, which marked a historic turning point and opened a broad road for human progress.

The Chilean armed forces' neutrality in October was no accident. It responded in the first place to the weight of tradition: institutionally and constitutionally they were subject to the executive power, that is, to President Allende. And in the second place to the putschist elements' relative weakness ever since the failure of Gen. Roberto Viaux's coup in October 1970, which led to the retirement of various implicated high officers and to acceptance of the constitutionalist "Schneider doctrine"

as dogma for the armed forces as a whole, represented by their commander-in-chief, Carlos Prats. Thirdly, it must be stressed that the
armed forces are not a stagnant organism, separated from and outside
of the class-structured social body. At the outset of the popular
government, most officers were already permeated by imperialist ideology, a considerable number were of middle-bourgeois extraction, and in
October 1972 their personal sympathies lay beyond a doubt with the
employer guilds. Of this there was evidence aplenty. Said Gen. Héctor
Bravo, chief of the Santiago zone during the state of emergency, on
October 26: "Citizens are informed that the undersigned has ordered
the public forces under his command to proceed to the immediate
eviction of all those who have occupied industries and enterprises."[6]
But the undersigned had to modify his orders next day to the effect
that they did not apply to industries whose owners had unilaterally
paralyzed their activities. A significant number of officers were vacillating, not merely because of their constitutional subordination to the
executive and because their commander-in-chief was loyal to President
Allende, but also and mainly because in October 1972 they could not
be sure of the compliance of all officers, NCOs, and privates in the face
of the workers' enthusiastic and determined organization and action
against the bourgeois insurrection.

Three never-to-be-repeated conditions existed in October 1972
which made revolutionary moves highly visible, given audacious and
resolute leadership: the extreme weakness of the bourgeoisie as a class
and of the state institutions in which they were entrenched; a people's
movement on the rise, cohesive, intensely active, and with embryos of
power as alternatives to traditional institutions; division and indecision
among the military, whose hands were tied by the concrete march of
events.

The possibility of deepening bourgeois-democratic legality was an
obvious alternative. In that case the scenario would have been to curtail
the power and maneuvering capacity of Congress, the courts, and the
comptroller's office which, now exposed as accessories in an abortive
plot, were retreating in search of new defense lines. It was the moment
to strike at them. Never a better opportunity to call a plebiscite on
points the government would decide, such as the formation of the
Social Production Sector, dissolution of Congress and creation of a
unicameral body, and democratization of the Supreme Court and other

juridical organs. Such a vigorous and decisive option taken after the defeat of the employers' associations would have been based on a class-alliance policy under proletarian leadership embracing campesinos, *pobladores,* public and private white-collar workers, small merchants and industrialists, artisans, professionals—all strata of the population whose interests were distinguishable from those of the middle and big bourgeoisie. The higher unity that such a policy and alliance could have forged would have permitted the program to advance toward fulfillment even within the "political road" framework. Not, of course, that such a policy could have solved all the problems faced by the Chilean process. We note only that it would have led the struggle between popular government and opposition, and between workers and bourgeoisie, to a new stage qualitatively more favorable to the former.

The third road—reaffirmation of the alliance with the "middle classes" as understood up until then—faced two main difficulties. One was the radicalization of the popular movement, which would have to be put back into the old institutional groove; the other was the Christian Democrats' repeated refusal, as representative of the "middle classes," to make a deal with the government. At the same time, the workers had come to see Christian Democracy as too implicated in the abortive October insurrection to be a valid interlocutor. Consequently, if implementation of the "politico-institutional road" policy was to go ahead under these new circumstances, it was necessary to find a new spokesman for those ambiguous and reticent "middle classes." So the policy was reformulated, bringing in a new element to permit implementation of the program within Chilean political tradition.

This was the road the government took with a new cabinet, installed on November 3, in which Gen. Carlos Prats became interior minister, Rear Admiral Ismael Huerta became minister of public works, and air force Brig. Gen. Claudio Sepúlveda took over the ministry of mining.

It is hard to plumb the depths of the intense discussions within Popular Unity about this political line chosen by President Allende. Various statements were made indicating profoundly negative reactions within the Socialist Party, many of whose regional committees publicly disagreed. The party's Central Committee unanimously rejected the line but bowed to it; the general secretary said the party had "never opposed inclusion of military men in the new cabinet," with a suggestive reference to "exclusive prerogatives of the president." CUT president and Communist Party Central Committee member Luis Figueroa, the new labor minister, took the opportunity to pronounce his opinions: "I believe the patriotic forces will assume the great responsibility of preventing paralysis of the country in order to consolidate the process and normalize national activities."

The formation of the new cabinet was received in the bourgeois camp with relief and optimism. With the armed forces present to guarantee the new equilibrium and to preserve the prevailing legality, the bourgeoisie could now retreat quietly and in good order. The following statements, all made on November 4, express this mood:

Senator Renán Fuentealba, Christian Democratic Party president: "I want to make clear that I think Gen. Carlos Prats possesses the combination of qualities to fulfill the delicate functions of interior minister. I will go further: we believe that, as a military man, he is better equipped than anyone to give assurance of impartial action." [7]

Senator Rafael Moreno, Christian Democrat: "The composition of the new cabinet constitutes a defeat for the most hard-line sectors of the government and the Socialist Party." [8]

Senator Francisco Bulnes, National Party: "On the one hand, the ministers from the armed forces would fully justify their entrance into the cabinet if their labors were oriented toward three great goals: restoring social peace, returning the government to legality, and assuring that the March elections are held under the untrammeled authority of civil liberties." [9]

El Mercurio editorial: "The latest statements by the army commander-in-chief [Carlos Prats, interior minister] satisfy the country's most heartfelt longings and particularly the democratic neutrality of the majority of Chileans."

General Prats: "We are called upon to collaborate with the government in the tasks it has set itself of ensuring social peace, gravely threatened by the dramatic patterns of the strike movement, and of seeing that the elections next March are held within the broadest guarantees for all sectors of opinion." [10]

On November 6 all the employer guilds gave instructions to end the strike movement. The attempted insurrection of October was defeated. For the moment.

1. *El Mercurio* (Santiago de Chile), October 8, 1972.
2. *El Mercurio,* October 11, 1972.
3. *El Mercurio,* October 13, 1972.
4. *El Mercurio,* October 21, 1972.
5. *El Mercurio,* October 28, 1972.
6. *El Mercurio,* October 26, 1972.
7. *El Mercurio,* November 4, 1972.
8. Ibid.
9. Ibid.
10. *Chile Hoy* magazine (Santiago de Chile), November 10, 1972.

6 POPULAR POWER

The history of Chile is the history of class struggle. During the Popular Unity government a people in combat set itself to end the centuries-old domination of the propertied classes and open the road to a new society; to destroy the traditional structures which kept rural and urban productive forces in a state of backwardness, perpetuated social and economic injustice, and anchored the country's most vital interests to imperialism.

In this struggle against the established system, the workers—for a time—counted on a strong bastion of support, the executive power which the Left parties won in the 1970 elections.

Yet historical experience and Marxist theory have shown how far the capture of the ruling class's state apparatus falls short of what is needed for the new tasks of transforming society; how indispensable it is, therefore, to destroy all the mechanisms regulating society during the rule of the bourgeoisie, if a new state based on the proletariat's ideological, economic, and political models is to be built.

Chilean history during the Popular Unity government is the history of a class struggle raised to a new level. What was then called into question was not only the capitalists' appropriation of surplus value produced by the proletariat but—much more important, and marking a qualitatively different stage—the whole position of the social classes, the right of the bourgeoisie to control economic and political relations.

In all successful transformation processes to date, the working class has emerged first as an embryonic power, then as an alternative power confronting the traditional dominant power, challenging, overturning, and obliterating it. This alternative power has always taken shape outside of institutional capitalist institutions and thus always as a qualitatively different model, not arising from within the bourgeois system but developing independently of it in a situation of general crisis for prevailing legality.

In the Chilean revolutionary process the Popular Unity government arose as a power confronting that of the bourgeoisie within the bourgeois-democratic institutional system. And what stood out in this process were the workers' level of independent revolutionary participation after October 1972 and the strategic objectives that characterized their program.

We must, however, bear in mind that different tendencies merged in the Popular Unity government. And that from the time of the Lo Curro agreements in June 1972, the Communist Party's Liberation Front theses predominated in the line that was followed. Consequently, the transformation objectives, which were of a tactical nature, acquired the status of a strategy; the popular movement had to go beyond the orientation provided for it by the government, and that contradiction made the whole process extremely confused with respect to the objectives and mechanisms of confrontation with capitalism.

The power of a social class resides in its capacity to institute its models of economic, ideological, and political domination. Undoubtedly Popular Unity's conquest of executive power seriously reduced the bourgeoisie's capacity to affirm and maintain its domination. But that executive power, as our account of its development has shown and will continue to show, was absolutely insufficient to confront the combined dominant forces, much less to promote and institute a new model that would assure a socialist future for Chile.

It was precisely from the month of June 1972, when the limitations of the "politico-institutional road" became evident and the executive found itself boxed in by the mechanisms that had permitted its accession to office, that the first—qualitatively new—expressions of worker organization independent of institutional structures emerged: the *cordones industriales.*

To understand how the *cordones* originated one needs to know something of the role of CUT, the trade-union confederation founded in 1953 under the militant presidency of Clotario Blest. With many Christian Democrats in its leadership, and under a labor code requiring a minimum of twenty-five workers to form a legal union, CUT always had a tough job getting the unions scattered around the country to affiliate on the basis of political pluralism. For these reasons, by 1972 CUT had only some 800,000 members out of some three million employed workers; for the same reasons, most of them were in big and middle industry and in state agencies. The general strike called by CUT in 1967 marked the beginning of an upward movement in labor, but there was a wave of strikes in 1970, 1971, and 1972 which were not always under CUT's control. Labor conflicts, averaging a thousand a year in 1967–1969, rose to 1,819 in 1970, 2,709 in 1971, and 1,763 in only the first half of 1972, showing the intensity of the class struggle. Furthermore, most of these strikes were not legal under code requirements and the average number of workers involved in each declined from 355 in 1970 to 108 in 1971 and the same in 1972.[1]

This record shows the massive involvement of middle- and small-enterprise blue- and white-collar workers and campesinos in the struggles historically carried on by workers joined in presenting demands of various kinds—mainly economistic—with CUT playing a secondary role, for the percentage of unionized strikers was only 22 in the first half of 1971, 26.6 in the second half, and 32.4 in the first half of 1972. So we see that throughout the period this large sector of workers in nonmonopolistic enterprises directed their energies toward getting a bigger share of national income—and to a great extent got it—although they showed, right up to the demise of the government, that they were not led by CUT.

All this emerged clearly in June 1972 when the first *cordón industrial* was born in Cerrillos. What happened there was that the workers of a middle-sized enterprise, the Perlak canning plant, went on strike for various demands and the firm refused to budge; they proceeded to occupy the plant, ousting bosses and managers and demanding the transfer of Perlak to the Social Production Sector. That was also the month of the Lo Curro meeting when Pedro Vuskovic, who had until then been minister of economy, was removed and the Communist Party line of class alliance with the middle bourgeoisie to "consolidate" previous gains was definitely confirmed as government policy. And that was the cue for Mireya Baltra, the Communist minister of labor, violently to reject the Perlak workers' demands and order the evacuation of the plant. At the same time the courts issued a second order for the plant to be restored to its owners, with the use of the police.

There were two basic reasons why CUT could not intervene. Firstly, although the May 1972 union elections had given Communists, Socialists, and Christian Democrats approximately equal strength in the organization, the decisive prevalence of Communists in its leadership and organizing apparatus made the going hard for any movement contrary to the tactical orientation of the Communists and the government. Secondly, the economistic struggles in which CUT had engaged until then gave it a correspondingly pyramidal structure based on industrial branches. In effect, the best organizational structure for putting forward wage, seniority, retirement, and work-condition demands is obviously that of grouping together workers with common problems arising from similarity of occupation.

But in the Perlak conflict the workers' goals far transcended these traditional ones: the issue was ownership of the enterprise. And on June 30 the Perlak workers, together with other workers in the area, gave their answer to the industry's owners, to institutional justice, and to the minister of labor: they occupied some plants, blocked access roads to the Maipú industrial area, and demonstrated their repudiation of the various institutions opposing their demands. Thus a new model of worker organization took shape, based on the common interests of workers in a given area and hence potentially different from the usual economic struggles, since their solidarity extended to general social problems other than the particular problems of a plant. The Cerrillos *cordón industrial* had been born. The experiment succeeded. Perlak was intervened; later it would be brought into the Social Production Sector and its workers would be among the most active and class-conscious in the community.

Cordones industriales developed strikingly during the great October confrontations. They sprang up in all the country's chief cities, and Santiago alone saw the emergence of five—O'Higgins, Vicuña Mackenna, San Joaquín, Cerrillos, and Recoleta—and later two more, Santiago Centro and Mapocho Cordillera. Each sector chose its leadership by direct vote of workers in the plants.

The orders of the day of the Vicuña Mackenna *cordón,* issued at a critical moment of the process, provide an example of *cordón* activities and goals:

1. Take over all industries.

2. Organize brigades of eleven compañeros with one as leader. Leaders of these brigades, together with trade-union leaders, will manage the industries.

3. Concentrate inside the plants the vehicles and materials required to defend the plant, the working class, and the government.

4. Plants will blow their sirens hourly to indicate that the situation is normal. In case of an abnormal situation sirens will be blown continuously to show that aid is needed, and thus it will be received. . . .

6. Keep tuned in to Radio Corporation [owned by the Socialist Party] . . . regardless of national network.

7. Station a watch at whatever point in the plant offers greatest visibility.

8. Maintain continuous contact with neighboring plants through compañeros acting as messengers.

9. The comando will function at. . . . If you can't get there until . . . , there will be leading *cordón* compañeros at. . . .

10. Organize assemblies and inform all compañeros of these instructions in each plant.[2]

In October the *cordones* were promoted mainly by members of MIR and MAPU. The role of the *cordones* was decisive in defeating the employer lockout and paralysis of the country. On the sector level they achieved effective coordination of the most important tasks: mobilization of workers, transport of raw materials and finished products, and liaison with community residents, especially with neighborhood *poblaciones* and *población* committees, in some cases with campesino councils of nearby farm areas. The coordination of security and control tasks in access streets was also effective.

Yet formation of the *cordones* was to a great extent instinctive, not in response to any Left party's plan. The Communist Party, seeing in them a danger of "parallelism" with CUT, and understandably fearing it could not channel them into its political line, instructed its members not to participate. The Socialist Party, while it called for building and strengthening the *cordones,* offered at the time no concrete plan for their organization beyond the sector limits and the spontaneity that characterized their birth. The *cordones* appeared on the scene as a rank-and-file response to the onslaught of the bourgeoisie, but also and mainly as a weapon for defense of the government.

When the employer strike ended early in November, the government turned the helm sharply to the right and the *cordones,* for lack of impetus from the Popular Unity parties, languished without concrete tasks despite the efforts of the MIR, which did not succeed in broadening its base in the industrial working class.

In January the *cordones* reacted strongly to the "Millas plan" which proposed to return to their owners many industries taken by the workers in October. The Socialist Party called for resistance to this policy of devolution and its newly invigorated cadres lined up the great majority of workers behind its position of "advance without compromise." January ended with demonstrations by the *cordones* to head off the "Millas plan," and it was withdrawn shortly afterwards since it could only have been implemented by using the repressive apparatus against *cordón*-organized workers.

But after this a new decline in *cordón* activity set in. The Socialist Party Plenum declared: "In all its forms of expression, but above all that of working-class control and leadership in the economic field, people's power must base itself on an institutional structure different from the traditional bourgeois one, with the government's support." This line clearly did not suffice to develop and gain ground for the *cordones,* which could play no major role if limited exclusively to the "economic field." Socialist Party directives between March 4 and the first military insurrection on June 29 were imprecise and unresponsive to the many functions that the *cordones* had shown they could perform.

Luis Corvalán spelled out the Communist Party position in a letter of February 7: "What must be supported is not the phantasmagoric 'people's power,' independent of the government, of which the MIR speaks and which exists only in the hot heads of its leaders, but the government of President Allende which is a concrete reality. . . ." Evolving this position later in an interview, Corvalán said: "In the particular case of the *cordones,* we see them as an integral part of CUT, as CUT rank-and-file organizations, not as parallel and divisive organizations of the labor movement."[3]

An abortive military coup took place in June; CUT and the government called on the workers to take over their plants as a defensive response, and the *cordones* entered a period of greater growth, clarity, and activity. The attempted sedition brought out all their energy:

> The Marxist strategy to win total control of industries and factories, which was broadened on June 29 with CUT's order to occupy plants—achieving 34,000 takeovers of enterprises, services, and workshops according to figures from the Economic Council of Ministers—places in Popular Unity's power a variety of means of production, many of which have been forcibly incorporated into the state sector.[4]

El Mercurio's figure is a clear exaggeration designed to provoke panic among small proprietors. A revolutionary process does not always provide all the time needed for correct statistics. But the point is that the workers did occupy most of the middle-sized and big industries in Santiago and other chief cities, and that the *cordones* were responsible for coordinating these actions.

By then experience made it possible to calculate the possibilities that were open and the explicit differences that existed between the *cordones industriales* and CUT. Thus we find in the weekly *La Aurora de Chile*—published by the Socialist Party's Central Santiago regional committee, the party's most important committee, and guided by Left revolutionary tendencies:

> (1) The CIs [*cordones industriales*] embrace new class groupings that are not in CUT: unaffiliated unions, nonunionized workers, employees in the tertiary sector. (2) The CI leadership is in the best geographical position to mobilize these and bring them together. (3) The CIs are not involved with bourgeois legality, while CUT is, through the unions and its new legal status. (4) CUT conveys an image of subordination to the government, which creates a certain suspicion in the working class, a fact skillfully exploited by the bourgeoisie in the last congressional elections; the CIs on the other hand were born out of the higher interests of the working class and visibly fight for the masses. (5) While the CIs permit great ideological pluralism in their ranks (including participation of Christian Democratic workers), they don't translate that participation into integration and power-sharing as does CUT, where a third of the leaders also belong to the leadership of the bourgeoisie. (6) The CIs aim to have the most representative leadership and hence attach great importance

to the sovereignty of each enterprise's Assembly in naming delegates to these workers' organizations. (7) Finally—and chiefly—the CIs are the only class organizations capable of becoming a territorial power in a situation of direct confrontation with the bourgeoisie, with all the strategic advantages that this signifies—advantages clearly demonstrated in recent situations. Therefore we believe that to the extent that they are not alternative organizations, the CIs and CUT can look toward working together in a mutually beneficial way which will serve to begin stimulating people's power throughout the country.[5]

In this same period the organic development of the *cordones* made possible an important step forward. At the end of July the Provincial Coordinating Board of the *cordones* in Santiago Province was formed, and elected as its president the Socialist Hernán Ortega, leader of the Vicuña Mackenna *cordón.* It outlined the following as the *cordones'* objectives:

(1) To defend and broaden the conquests of the government and working class; (2) to provide direct democratic representation for *cordón* workers; (3) to constitute themselves as organs of defense of the present government to the extent that it represents the workers' interests; (4) to deepen the process and sharpen class contradictions; (5) to fight for broader participation of the working class in decisions affecting its interests, and build the power of unions and working-class organizations; (6) to cooperate decisively in organizing and preparing sector defense organizations, so that territorial and political control may be assured to the working class.[6]

This was to be the Chilean workers' last organizational and creative effort to confront bourgeois reaction. Less than two months later the military coup would smash the scanty resistance concentrated in a few dozen big factories and some *campamentos* and *poblaciones.* The disproportion of arms was so enormous that, wherever there was no vacillation in the ranks of the armed forces, the *cordón* defense organization proved totally ineffective. Nevertheless, the record stands that in practice the *cordones* constituted a completely autonomous power vis-à-vis the government and all institutions of the Chilean capitalist state—a power which developed in a qualitatively new way the consciousness and influence of the working class in the sectors where the *cordones* existed; which impeded the growth of a state bureaucracy beyond worker control; and which broadened worker participation in the administration of enterprises. In the geographic localities the capacity to provide leadership proved extremely weak and only became a reality in particular cases; yet the germ of democratic and independent worker power with a revolutionary organizational perspective was shown to be much more real than "phantasmagoric." In light of the popular parties' declarations and directives we can say that the workers' capacity to rise out of the class struggle's legalistic quagmire did exist and did develop. And that it was the vacillations of their political organizations, and the limitations of the "institutional road," that prevented their crystallization into a power which was a real alternative to the power of the bourgeoisie.

The *cordones* were not the only new organizational element generated by the workers during Chile's revolutionary process. Although more limited, in the development of that process *comandos comunales* (neighborhood commands) and *consejos comunales campesinos* (campesino communal councils) were also created.

The *comandos comunales* brought together industrial workers through representatives of unions or *cordones;* representatives of the sector's *poblaciones* and *campamentos;* women mainly through the JAPs (Supply and Price Committees); agricultural unions; in some cases student centers; and representatives of revolutionary Left parties. But first we must note the antecedents in Chile of popular-participation organizations: neighborhood committees, mothers' centers, student centers, *población* committees, campesino unions.

Chile's relatively early industrialization and urbanization, working-class organization and struggle, the growth of an important white-collar sector of public employees, the absence of sharp conflicts between the different bourgeois groups, the stability and capacity of capitalist state institutions during most of this century—all these permitted the development in Chile of diverse bourgeois-democratic forms that had deepened their roots in recent years and that also found expression in the existence of mass-based organizations of popular representation.

It was during the six-year Frei regime that the neighborhood committees (*juntas de vecinos*) were created; legalized in 1968, they numbered 3,487 by 1970. They were supposed to concern themselves with problems of the neighborhood or *población,* all of whose inhabitants participated. In effect they came into being mainly in popular sectors and gave rise to periodic neighborhood elections in which Christian Democracy gained majority influence. Neighborhood bigwigs were prominent in them—that is, businessmen, professionals, small proprietors, all those who according to prevailing ideology stood out from the amorphous mass—which explains why they became bastions of Christian Democratic reformism. At the same time, especially in the *poblaciones,* the Frei government promoted mothers' centers which reached a total of 6,000.[7] The mothers' centers were supposed to rationalize the preparation of meals, teach and encourage knitting—in brief, to define and limit even more clearly the functions "proper" to woman and strengthen her conservative role in Chilean society.

Christian Democratic strategy also made skillful approaches to the urban population's broad dispossessed sector, the "homeless ones," who were organized in *población* committees outside of trade-union struggles and thus could more easily be won for a reformist policy. Reformism achieved considerable influence by channeling these people's aspirations into the acquisition of housing and subsequently into improvement of the neighborhood infrastructure. At the start of the Popular Unity government, around 55,000 families were living in *campamentos*—that is, 10 percent of Greater Santiago's population[8]— and in May 1972 the housing ministry reported 83,000 families in *campamentos*—that is, 15 percent. This huge popular sector had begun to be influenced by the Left parties since the Frei government's last years—in bitter battles with Christian Democratic officials—when those parties helped organize illegal takeovers of empty lots in which *campamento* and *población* dwellers settled, and subsequently led their struggles to obtain basic living needs. This coincided with the growing economic difficulties of the last Frei years, due to which fiscal resources and consequent solutions to the housing problem had greatly declined; hence the Christian Democratic government stiffened its attitude toward takeovers of land, culminating in a massacre of *pobladores* in Puerto Montt in 1969. Thus the *población* committees in 1971-1972 saw a growing influence of Socialists, Communists, and Miristas, who generally replaced Christian Democrats as committee leaders.[9]

The JAPs were first proposed at a meeting of Minister of Economy Vuskovic with housewives in July 1971. At the first signs of shortages at the end of that year, the Communist Party encouraged the formation of the committees and in April 1972 the government gave them legal status by promulgating a decree sent for review to the comptroller's office. The JAPs had the following aims: control of prices and hoarding, easement of supply, consumer education, and antibureaucratic struggle. These were advisory rather than executive tasks since the JAPs' activities were limited, in the case of hoarding for example, to denunciations to the authorities; they were not authorized to take any other action. The fact is that the government had drafted a decree with a different content, but the comptroller's office objected on the ground that any government initiative granting executive powers must be approved by Congress. During October 1972 the JAPs largely transcended the "advisory" role and did much to stop hoarding and the closings of commercial establishments. Their effectiveness corresponded to their growth: in January 1973 there were more than 2,100 JAPs in the country, with more than 1,000 spread through 34 districts of Santiago,[10] and the number grew to 2,500 in March.[11] From the second half of 1972 shortages were one of the chief issues in the class struggle, hence the importance of the JAPs, which became a substantial weapon of the popular sectors.

In the *campamentos,* and to a lesser extent in the *poblaciones,* alternative forms of distribution were developed—direct supply in which state food distributors played a big role. Two original mechanisms were created: the "people's food basket" which was delivered to People's Stores (the first of these appeared in the Lo Hermida *población* in December 1972) for direct distribution among the inhabitants through the JAPs, and direct supply from the state distributors' mobile supermarkets. JAP participants were mainly Popular Unity women and their activities were always strenuously opposed by the bourgeoisie, who sought with considerable success to set the JAPs against established shopkeepers. Nevertheless, during 1973 they were an indispensable reality to assure purchasing power to broad popular strata, and they won broad sectors of women to support of the government.

Student centers have existed in Chile since the second decade of this century, and selfless youth has repeatedly shown its readiness for sacrifice and for devotion to the workers' cause. But the class polarization that occurred in Chile moved broad strata of students of "middle-class" extraction into opposition to the Popular Unity government. During 1973 secondary and university students were deeply divided, so that we find certain centers joining hands with *población* committees in the tasks of building popular power while others simultaneously occupied units of the universities and demonstrated violently against the government.

The first call to organize *comandos comunales* came during the People's Assembly at Concepción in July 1972. But the violent criticism this evoked from the Communist Party and from President Allende, as well as the censure of the Concepción regional committee by the central committee of the Socialist Party, prevented fulfillment of the initiative except embryonically in scattered communities. It was during the October employer strike that the *comandos* were developed parallel with the *cordones,* with the already mentioned organizations participating: unions, *población* committees, Left political parties in their respective zones, JAPs, student centers and other neighborhood groups, and in some cases campesino organizations. What mainly motivated the formation of the *comandos* was without doubt the desire to carry through tasks that the state apparatus was not able to, due to the dislocation resulting from the bourgeois insurrection and the government's defense against such attacks. The primary goals were to assure continuation of work in industry in face of the employer lockout, which meant assuring the functioning of the plant despite the absence of bosses and often of technicians; to regulate delivery of the various raw materials and channel the distribution of what was produced; to mobilize public transportation, institute a whole new system of food distribution both to workers in the enterprises and to *campamento* and *población* inhabitants; and to form health councils which would meet basic medical needs when most doctors and technicians had abandoned their responsibilities. Finally, to implement measures of protection and security against sabotage by the terrorist groups of right-wing organizations and parties.

Thus we see converging in the workers' *comandos comunales* different social sectors and strata: big-industry workers along with workers in middle and small enterprises; *pobladores* who for the most part were unskilled construction workers; unemployed; self-employed; white-collar state employees, especially in the health and teaching fields; students; campesinos in the land-reform sector; and small landowning farmers. Altogether some one hundred *comandos* were formed,[12] of which about twenty were in Greater Santiago, the rest scattered through Valparaíso, Concepción, Ñuble, Cautín, and Linares provinces. Some idea of their composition can be had from a document of the Coordinating Committee for the Northern Area, recording the participation of twenty-one mass organizations: four *pobladores,* three in big plants, two of campesinos, two of students, and the rest in small plants and workshops.[13]

We have already noted the basic reasons for the birth of the *comandos comunales.* But immediately after the rout of the employer strike, the government appeared to strengthen itself through the inclusion of military chiefs, and the state apparatus resumed normal functioning, even if with great supply problems; so the *comandos* began to decline, even more than the *cordones.*

After the attempted *tancazo** at the end of June 1973 the *comandos comunales* were reactivated, but here again we find important differences of political evaluation: while the MIR particularly attempted to strengthen the *comandos,* the left revolutionary tendencies in the Socialist Party preferred to support efforts to develop the *cordones,* deeming it indispensable to assure working-class hegemony first before moving on to new organic forms into which other popular strata would be drawn. That is, the Socialists did not oppose development of the *comandos* but gave priority to more solid implantation of the *cordones.* Thus they said the following in the journal *Tarea Urgente,* organ of the newly constituted organizations, basically sparked by Socialists of the Cordillera regional committee in Santiago: "Today more than ever the nation's political situation requires the development and creation of new forms of popular power, the creation of *cordones industriales* and, once these are completely structured and functioning, the constitution of *comandos comunales* as the highest expression of class power. In this way we will develop a popular power that will prove irreversible."[14]

But time was no longer on the side of Chilean society's revolutionary forces. The experience was cut off before popular consciousness and organizing capacity had fully developed.

* A word coined at the time, referring to the fact that the coup attempt was led by tank corps.

At the end of 1970 the government had sent to the comptroller's office a decree creating the campesino communal councils in which were to participate the agricultural unions (three at that time), representatives of cooperatives of the respective communes (small landowning campesinos), and representatives of the *asentados* (campesinos of lands expropriated during the Frei regime). Under Decree No. 481 as reviewed by the comptroller's office early in 1971, the campesino councils' prerogatives were merely consultative and informative in matters related to policies on agrarian reform, prices, credit, trade, taxes, etc. However, during 1971 and with even greater force in 1972 the class war had firmly rooted itself in the Chilean countryside. The number of unionized campesinos had climbed from 100,000 to 140,000 during 1970, and by the end of 1971 reached 210,000.[15]

Campesinos often lacked the necessary patience to carry out the agrarian reform in an orderly and methodical way. In spite of the organs responsible for implementing it, takeovers of agricultural lands kept spiralling from the end of 1970 through 1971: 148 in 1969, 456 in 1970, 1,278 in 1971.[16] On the one hand, these takeovers responded to the campesinos' yearning to get rid of the big-estate employers and so obtain more returns from their labor, but on many occasions there was a deep contradiction with the agrarian-reform law, since it reserved for the landowner the equivalent of eighty irrigated hectares of land and ownership of all cattle, machinery, buildings, silos, etc. In many takeovers—promoted first by the MIR and later also by the Socialist Party and MAPU—the campesinos sought to override these guarantees to the powerful rural middle bourgeoisie. Faced with this situation the government speeded implementation of the agrarian reform, carefully avoiding use of the public forces which the courts were demanding. As a result of this violent and harsh awakening of campesino and rural-proletariat consciousness and organization, the big landlords, lacking their usual support from the state repressive apparatuses, organized themselves throughout Chile to defend their threatened property. Thus the National Agricultural Society called on landowners to "repel by use of legitimate defense any attack, threatening their persons or properties, for the purpose of occupying or taking over lands whether their own or those of neighbors."[17]

In this situation of dislocation of the state apparatus, the campesino councils also overrode their formal limitations and, mainly impelled by Socialists, Mapucistas, and Miristas, constituted themselves democratically with representatives from the rank and file, that is, with representation proportionate to the commune's social composition. One study shows that the leadership in 27 percent of the councils was predominantly rural-proletarian, in 15 percent *asentados,* in 16 percent small proprietors, and in 42 percent a combination of forces.[18] This composition would change later when it was precisely landless campesinos and *asentados* who organized councils to confront the reactionary counteroffensive.

At the end of 1971 the campesino council of Linares Province, together with the Popular Unity and MIR regional committees, issued a document which reflected a marked advance in the goals set by these popular-power organisms. Among their demands were the following: "Immediate elimination of latifundia. Expropriation of entailed estates. Reduction from eighty to forty hectares of the limit of nonexpropriable land. Expropriated land not to be compensated. No to the landowner's right of reserve. . . . Build the campesino councils."[19]

The *consejos comunales campesinos* extended to almost all of Chile's agricultural provinces, but their ability to make decisions varied with conditions. In zones where the demands were strongest, the councils were radicalized and moved on from advisory to executive tasks, planning estate takeovers, and demanding removal of government agrarian officials as well as developing plans for grain and cattle production, and formulating product-sales policies.[20] However, this level was not always reached. In Chile's countryside the councils were an embryo of effective power which experienced a rapid process of consolidation and consciousness of new goals.

We have tried to show the level of organization and capacity for action reached by different forms of popular power in Chile during the revolutionary process. Here it should also be noted that there was no unanimity about the relations between the government and this popular power. The Communist Party, which after the June 1973 military insurrection lukewarmly supported development of popular power, emphatically insisted on its necessary linkages with, dependence on, and complementary relation to the government. The other Popular Unity parties took less forthright positions but in general none attempted to use this power to challenge the government. The most categorical stance was taken by the MIR, which came out strongly for total independence from "all bourgeois institutionality," including by implication the executive power. The left wing of the Socialist Party for its part always saw the popular government as an indispensable mainstay for development of the revolutionary process and confrontation with the bourgeoisie.

Certainly the government never opposed the popular movement in Chile. However, the limitations imposed by its subordination to the institutional system created and perfected by the bourgeoisie never permitted it to become a dynamic force in the development of new popular-power organization. On the contrary, beginning in June 1972 the first signs appeared of a class alliance which was not favorable to working-class initiative, and subsequently the Prats-Millas cabinet objectively became a brake upon the organizations created by the workers in October. Later, Socialist Gerardo Espinoza would declare on taking office as interior minister: "Acts of force or violence, wherever they may originate, will not be accepted by the interior minister. Nor will we allow 'takeovers' to become the normal thing."[21]

The fact is that Chile had displayed a series of special characteristics clearly differentiating it from other Latin American countries: in the first place the strength of Chilean civic institutions, which had permitted deepening of democratic gains without ever endangering the foundations of the system—for the various dominant bourgeois strata and important sectors of the state bureaucracy alike found in that system the necessary ways of expressing their interests and participating in determination of the national income. This had limited the aspirations of the armed forces, which had to be content with the role of relatively second-string guardians of the regime. The development of Chile's industry meant a corresponding growth of trade unions and a union federation with strong independent traditions. At the same time, the subordination of most of the economy to big foreign concerns would impart to the recovery of Chile's basic resources the obvious character of a national demand. But although they made possible an advanced bourgeois-democratic state, all these characteristics made no qualitative change in the essence of the system, which continued to be capitalist and deeply dependent, inasmuch as the Chilean bourgeoisie was subjected, in its chief aspects, to the world capitalist system. To start with, it depended on the capitalist market in its production of copper; then it had to supply itself with machinery and technology, mainly from the United States; and furthermore, it obtained its credits and loans from the same source. Consequently it was indispensable for the bourgeoisie, monopolist or otherwise, to maintain its ties with world capitalism.

In November 1970 the workers' parties penetrated to the dynamic heart of Chile's institutional system. But progressively, as they tried to implement their program of reducing bourgeois economic power and transferring it to a state with Popular Unity controlling the presidency, the institutional mechanisms managed by the dominant class through its control of the other state centers (Congress, courts, comptroller) and its influence in the armed forces—along with its always decisive economic hold—permitted that class to hamstring the executive power. This was not realized in time by Popular Unity and particularly by President Allende and the Communist Party, who tried to maintain to the end a suicidal legality which braked development of a new worker institutionality to counter that of the bourgeoisie. The government repudiated and criticized the Concepción Popular Assembly, hampered the development of *cordones* and *comandos,* damped down and subdued the workers' initiative. Due to its origin and perspective it at no time put itself in the vanguard in the creation of new organic forms of real popular power. On the contrary. In these circumstances, given the objective level reached by the process and the institutional strength of the bourgeoisie, the workers found themselves at a given moment defending the government—but the government was no longer their chief base of support and they could not count on it although they had to continue looking to it. They faced two alternative roads which, while not counterposed, were divergent: popular government and popular power.

This being so, we cannot be surprised that the workers' creativity should have been limited by the state apparatus and that, when institutionality emerged as a clearly reactionary force, the workers were not capable of overriding it and realizing the full potential of the embryonic forms of alternative power. In other words, when from the first July days of 1973 the institutional forces showed themselves diametrically opposed to the needs of the government and the popular movement, the popular parties, the working class and its allies, along with the state apparatus controlled by executive power, could not suddenly alter their course and tactics—for the whole previous process had conditioned their development and limited their action to the modalities of capitalist legality.

The possibilities inherent in all the various forms of popular power never escaped the bourgeoisie. A large part of its ideological campaign was directed against the campesino councils, JAPs, and *cordones,* and in support of the Nationalists' and Christian Democrats' repeated demands for observance of the Arms Control Law. Thus Senate president Eduardo Frei declared in July:

> . . . Orders have been given to occupy factories and rural estates; the *cordones industriales* with which it is hoped to surround the city have been reinforced; and what is more serious, it is certain that arms are being distributed, strategic positions taken up, and instructions issued as if Chile were on the brink of civil war. The so-called popular power is not the people of Chile. It is political groups who describe themselves as the people and who aim to subjugate other workers by force, without hesitating to use any means of achieving it.[22]

This monumental appeal to counter-revolutionary cant was made only a few days after the frustrated attempt at the military coup known as the *tancazo,* and two months before the September 11 putsch which would bring bloody destruction to the people of Chile and their organizations. Frei recognized the chief obstacle to his program of "national reconstruction": popular power.

1. Emir Sader, *Movilización de Masas y Sindicalización en el Gobierno de la UP,* Santiago de Chile, mimeo, 1973.
2. *Chile Hoy* magazine (Santiago de Chile), July 6, 1973.
3. *Chile Hoy,* April 12, 1973.
4. *El Mercurio* (Santiago de Chile), April 12, 1973.
5. The weekly *La Aurora de Chile* (Santiago de Chile), No. 35, July 26, 1973, cited in Maurice Najmann, *Le Chili Est Proche* (Paris: Maspéro, 1974).
6. *Chile Hoy,* July 27, 1973.
7. Presidential report, May 1970.
8. Duque and Pastrana, "La Movilización Reivindicativa Urbana de los Sectores Populares en Chile," *Revista Latinoamericana de Ciencias Sociales* (Santiago de Chile), No. 4.
9. Pastrana and Threlfall, *Pan, Techo y Poder* (Buenos Aires: Ediciones SIAP, 1974).
10. *Chile Hoy,* January 19, 1973.
11. *Chile Hoy,* March 9, 1973.
12. *Chile Hoy,* December 8, 1972.

13. Pastrana and Threlfall, *Pan, Techo y Poder.*
14. *Tarea Urgente* (Santiago de Chile), No. 13, August 22, 1973.
15. Fondo de Extensión y Educación Sindical (FEES), Santiago de Chile, mimeo.
16. E. Klein, Instituto de Capacitación e Investigación en Reforma Agraria (ICIRA), Santiago de Chile, mimeo, 1972.
17. *El Mercurio,* May 8, 1973.
18. Gómez and E. Klein, ICIRA, Santiago de Chile, mimeo, April 1972.
19. *El Rebelde* (Santiago de Chile), weekly organ of the MIR, No. 11, December 13, 1971.
20. Resolutions of the Second Campesino Council Congress, Cautín Province.
21. *El Mercurio,* March 29, 1973.
22. *El Mercurio,* July 8, 1973.

7 MARCH 1973: THE "PARLIAMENTARY ROAD" OF THE RIGHT

In Chile's early nineteenth-century struggles for independence, a young revolutionary and popular leader, José Miguel Carrera, struck a telling blow for his country's liberty. The historian Francisco Encina relates this significant event at the end of 1812: "Since the main resistance came from the Congress, Carrera decided to dissolve it without more ado. With the force at his command this was certainly not difficult. He lined up some cannons in front of the hall where the deputies sat, ringed the plaza with three battalions, and gave orders that no one could leave. In the face of this open coercion, the president and ten deputies signed the writ suspending the Congress and transferring all its powers to the executive."

Nothing of the kind occurred in the battle of Chile's "second independence" in 1972. What was then on the agenda were the March 1973 parliamentary elections. Certainly the Congress had become the main obstacle to the transformations projected by the executive, but decisive action to do away with it was the last thing on the mind of Popular Unity. The most that was contemplated was to modify it with a new constitution. Thus, the bourgeois insurrection having ended in defeat, the government proceeded to transform the popular victory into semi-victory. Among the various possible alternatives at the end of October 1972, the choice that was made caused widespread surprise: to bring representatives of the armed forces into the new cabinet, with the declared aim of ensuring "social peace" and enabling the March elections to take place democratically.

During 1972 there was a marked intensification of social conflict, culminating in the great confrontations we have observed. The "dialogue" with Christian Democracy was broken off and there was no way of renewing it in the near future. The mechanisms for coordinating the different institutions had lost most of their flexibility, and state regulatory organs clashed constantly on all points at issue. In other words, the Chilean institutional system had run out of gas.

In that situation President Allende revised the tactic hitherto followed and, since the political representatives of social classes could find no basis of agreement, turned to the military for a consensus which would permit the government to pursue its program and socioeconomic relations to be reorganized. This new plan was based on the belief that the political parties, particularly Christian Democracy, could be edged out as defenders of the "middle classes" and directly integrated into an alliance which the government itself would lead, underpinned by the military presence in administrative decisions.

From that moment the military emerged as the predominant force in the Chilean state, and at least for a time would play an arbiter role in the class struggle that rocked the nation. However, the dynamic of that struggle and deep contradictions in the economy would in short order dispel the illusions based on their participation.

The new government essentially pivoted on the interior minister, Gen. Carlos Prats, responsible for maintaining civil order, and the minister of economy, Communist Orlando Millas, responsible for implementing the much delayed project of alliance with middle entrepreneurs.

The former's task was relatively easy: the pre-election period between November 1972 and early March 1973 was marked by no more violence than similar previous periods in a country like Chile. The freedoms of assembly, association, press, demonstration, and propaganda were fully assured and were exercised according to the means at the disposal of the various organizations. The military presence imposed its weight.

In the matter of regulating social interests, Millas sent to Congress the bill known as the "Millas Plan" or "Prats-Millas Plan," dated January 24, redefining the three types of property in Chile. In this it was proposed to transfer forty-nine enterprises to the social sector, guaranteeing the owners adequate compensation through creation of an appeals tribunal in which nominees of the courts would participate. A more important proposal under the plan was the return to their former owners of no less than 123 enterprises which had been in their workers' hands since October. As the bill put it, "The government has further resolved to hasten the solution of problems arising in other enterprises which were not in the social sector and which, due to various matters and conflicts, have been intervened or requisitioned. . . . With a view to creating conditions which will permit the earliest possible resolution of such situations, the rapid formulation of adequate measures has been ordered."[1]

Thus the whole sweeping advance that the workers, in defeating the bourgeoisie in October, had made in the battle for ownership of the means of production was nullified by a cold bureaucratic measure designed to stop them in their tracks and to guarantee, all over again, the interrupted march of capitalism in Chile.

As a proof of "good will," Millas proposed the return to its former owners of the electric-appliances enterprises in Arica. The heart of the new cabinet's task was to "consolidate" the process. But the class-struggle dynamic could not be so easily stopped with administrative measures and parliamentary bills. The furor provoked by these measures led to an immediate response by the *cordones industriales.* On January 30 thousands of workers, led by Socialists, Miristas, and Mapucistas, demonstrated in downtown Santiago their repudiation of the new cabinet's conciliatory policy with shouts of "Power to the Workers!" and the demand that no enterprise be returned to its owners.

The Socialist Party played a vital role in this mobilization. Responding to the interests of the new wave of members recruited in the October days, Carlos Altamirano said: "With the same moral authority that makes it compañero Allende's duty to criticize the workers when they fail in their responsibilities in social-sector enterprises, the workers and campesinos have an equal right to criticize the government when it commits errors."[2]

In a letter addressed to the Communist Party, Altamirano went much further in his criticism:

> The policy that compañero Orlando Millas, minister of economy, has put before the country objectively offers new guarantees to the bourgeoisie and the parties representing it. . . . The new plan reduces, for the moment, the number of monopolistic and strategic enterprises in the social sector, and offers the owners much more favorable compensation than the previous one. . . . It proposes the return of enterprises requisitioned or intervened due to labor problems and even to acts of sabotage by the owners.[3]

In the polemic aroused by this policy of conciliating the bourgeoisie, President Allende defended the "Millas Plan"; the Socialist Party responded by stating that its political commission "knew the terms in which it was conceived and categorically rejected them."

What is surprising is that just when the government was pursuing a clear policy of rapprochement with business circles, keeping order and "social peace" with the armed forces' assistance, applying the brakes to popular organs like the *cordones*—in a word, taking a line of substantial retreat with respect to the program and making no less substantial concessions to the opposition and bourgeoisie—the Socialist Party remained the principal organization in Popular Unity, and Socialists Clodomiro Almeyda, Hernán Del Canto, and Rolando Calderón continued to function in tandem with the rest of the cabinet of which they were members. The explanation of this seeming contradiction lies in the government's coherence and homogeneity and the Socialist Party's heterogeneity and inconsistency.

The Socialist Party had a long history of service to popular causes and on April 19, 1973, celebrated its fortieth anniversary as the principal organization of Chilean workers. But that history is also marked by the coexistence within the party of diverse currents: Marxist revolutionary, petty-bourgeois revolutionary, petty-bourgeois reformist, and bourgeois-reformist tendencies. After its Eleventh Congress in 1947 it entered a period of greater programmatic and ideological definition, and its strategy—purged of the bourgeois-reformist element, which was expelled—came to be based on the reorganization of its members and denunciation of the Chilean propertied class as an ally of imperialism and an enemy of change. Its Chillán and Linares congresses confirmed this tendency and in 1967 it proclaimed:

> The Socialist Party, as a Marxist-Leninist organization, declares the taking of power as the strategic goal to be achieved by this generation, to establish a revolutionary state which will liberate Chile from dependency and from economic and cultural backwardness and begin construction of socialism.
>
> Revolutionary violence is inevitable and legitimate. It necessarily results from the repressive and armed character of the class state. It is the only road to the capture of political and economic power and to the subsequent defense and strengthening of that power. Only by destroying the bureaucratic and military apparatus of the bourgeois state can the socialist revolution be consolidated. . . .

The Workers' Front policy champions unity of action by proletariat, campesinos, and poor middle classes, under leadership of the former. The Workers' Front is fortified by incorporation of revolutionary student and intellectual sectors into the political struggle for socialism. . . .

We postulate the class independence of the Workers' Front, seeing that the national bourgeoisie is allied to imperialism and is in fact its instrument; thus it has ended by becoming irreversibly counter-revolutionary.[4]

This line did not, however, eliminate various divisive tendencies among both middle cadre and top leadership; so that despite the positions taken at its congresses, the Socialist Party was notable for its inconsistency. In 1971 the Twenty-third Congress at La Serena took a new leftward turn: "Popular Unity's victory in entering a basic branch of the state opens vast perspectives for reaching the workers' goal of taking power and beginning to build socialist society. But capture of the presidency of the Republic in the framework of bourgeois institutionalism does not suffice to produce automatic passage from a bourgeois to a workers' government."[5] And on the eve of the March 1973 elections the party's general secretary said: "Let us not forget that we are experiencing not a revolution but a revolutionary process. A process we have to intensify because otherwise we run the risk of not having a revolution. Indeed we might end up without a revolutionary process."[6]

But these declarations were not translated into corresponding practice. Deeply rooted as it was in the masses and receptive to their changing drives, the Socialist Party never managed to unify its leadership and challenge President Allende's and the Communist Party's policy except on rare occasions. This explains why at important junctures the Popular Unity and government leadership always came up with a majority in strong disagreement with official Socialist Party declarations. The party's petty-bourgeois, technocratic, and reformist sectors invariably allied themselves with the tendencies, orientations, and tactics which they shared with other forces outside the party.

For its part the government was quite cohesive under the president's leadership and the fact that it contained Socialists—chosen not by the party but by Allende—was no obstacle. In the face of the violent October confrontation which threatened to throw its political line overboard, the government opted for slowing down the class struggle and taking the class-alliance policy to its ultimate consequences. Thus the defeat of the bourgeoisie was minimized, and the military could enter a cabinet which would extend bourgeois-democratic liberties, maintaining all the rights and institutions inherent in the capitalist system, sending to Congress a bill to reduce the scope of the social sector, and setting future ground rules that institutionally disarmed the workers and killed expectation of significant advances. The Socialist Party protested but went along, due to the relationship of forces between different tendencies in its Central Committee, which basically favored following the Communist Party line.

MIR correctly assessed the dangers of putting that policy into effect. Its general secretary, Miguel Enríquez, was quoted in *El Mercurio* of March 15, 1973: "For some months now they [Popular Unity] have joined in promoting a policy whose general content tends to consolidate social peace and the bourgeois order." Despite this accurate diagnosis, MIR was unable to influence the day-to-day struggle; its influence in the organized working class was very small, and not much greater among workers in general.

MIR was founded in August 1965 in the leather and shoe workers' headquarters, as a result of the convergence of diverse sectors. Its first general secretary, Dr. Enrique Sepúlveda, sought to develop this vigorous movement by combining the impetus provided by the Cuban Revolution with the proletarianization of its membership. In the end it was the *foco* tendencies inspired by Che Guevara's actions, with a student base, that prevailed at MIR's second congress. From that time, December 1967, MIR went all-out to militarize itself under Miguel Enríquez's leadership, and this resulted in almost total failure to root itself in the working class. Allende's victory in 1970 took MIR by surprise and it played a very limited role in the events of October 1972. Determination, heroism, and clarity were simply not enough. No revolution can make headway outside of the masses and MIR's elitist concept of political organization prevented it from ever winning significant influence in the labor movement.

MAPU was likewise a small if very active force. Torn by two contradictory tendencies that effectively neutralized it—one cleaving to the revolutionary Left, the other developing bourgeois-reformist positions—it split in two in the first days of March 1973, further weakening its limited capacity for action. Trying to become the effective left wing of Popular Unity, it propounded some sound tactics and policies but could make no mark on the course of events.

The Communist Party, on the contrary, enjoyed great homogeneity and powerful influence in the labor and popular movements. It had a fifty-year tradition and the continuity of its strategic line and leadership levels was noteworthy. Its Popular Front line was propounded and put into practice in 1938, when with the party's support a representative of the "national bourgeoisie" became president of Chile. In 1948 another member of the Radical Party, President Gabriel González Videla, suppressed the party and thus closed the cycle of collaboration on the government level. Subsequently the Communists developed the National Liberation Front strategy, envisaging an alliance between the "nonimperialist bourgeoisie" and the workers to stimulate the productive forces and transform the country's economy. This was basically the policy adopted during the Popular Unity government. The party's leadership was no less stable than its policy and in 1973 it had the same general secretary, Luis Corvalán, as in 1958. Its concept of the transfer of power from one social class, the bourgeoisie, to a new alliance in which the proletariat would be determinant, was essentially gradualist and evolutionary, envisaging the possibility not only of taking power by an "unarmed road" but of reaching that goal step by step: first the executive, then a parliamentary majority, then economic power, followed by transformation of the judiciary, finally arriving at a socialist and pluralist society. This concept remained unmodified throughout the process and was fully reflected in positions further elaborated and defined by Allende.

The new period initiated by the Prats-Millas cabinet reflected the deep skepticism of Popular Unity's decisive sectors as to the possibility of transforming state structures by the workers' energy and will, and outside of prevailing institutionality. Consequently they thought there would be no antagonism between the popular government and the state's coercive forces, so long as the values of the small and middle propertied bourgeoisie were not harmed. The Chilean process was supposed to affect only the interests of imperialism and of the big monopolist bourgeoisie. The new cabinet, the participation of the armed forces, and the Millas Plan for the three areas of the economy were the precise expression of these objectives.

But simultaneously with the growth of social struggles and their political expression, the country had veered from the traditional economic path. Of course there had been no qualitative change: despite the great growth of the state sector and the bourgeoisie's consequent loss of power, this class still played the key role and the capitalist market's rules of supply and demand remained in full force. It became clear during the October days that the bourgeoisie controlled most of the Chilean economy. The popular government had moved toward a real redistribution of national income and the social sector embraced a sizable part of production and services. However, the government was far from controlling them and, furthermore, was particularly weak in the area of imports and distribution. By conviction and the need to respond to the popular sectors forming its social base, the government's policy tended first to increase and then to maintain the purchasing power of wage-earners. In this situation shortages of many articles had arisen, partly through insufficient production but also, since the end of 1972, through the massive diversion of capital to hoarding and speculation by all the propertied strata. Partly from material interest and partly by political decision, the increase of investment in production did not materialize and capital was concentrated in distribution.

Economic aggression by imperialism played a far from minor role. On December 4, 1972, Salvador Allende said in the United Nations: "The plunge of world copper prices in the last twelve months has meant to a country with little more than $1 billion of exports a loss in income approximating $200 million."[7] Allende went on to point out that the World Bank, the Inter-American Development Bank, and the Agency for International Development had suspended traditional credits to the tune of some $130 million, and private U.S. banks' short-term credit lines had been suspended to the tune of $220 million. Furthermore, various agencies such as the Export-Import Bank were demanding payment in advance of the previous government's commitments. All of this dramatically affected the balance of payments in Chile, whose economy remained deeply dependent on the world capitalist system. During that visit, and also on his visit to the Soviet Union in 1972, Allende sought to broaden his margin of action in this field. The results were not as expected. As Foreign Minister Clodomiro Almeyda told it: "A commitment was obtained from the Soviet Union to contribute to supplying our country . . . for a volume of some $30 million. The USSR agreed to the consolidation or postponement of credit lines in convertible currency and foreign currency which were obtained last year for a total of $103 million." Almeyda also said that most of the disposable Soviet credits were arranged during the Frei period.[8] The truth is that these Soviet contributions to Chile's balance of payments under the popular government were absolutely insufficient, not only to break the country's dependency on the centers of world capitalism but to keep the sinking economy afloat. Certainly there were no previous commitments on the Soviet Union's part; they only reflected a political option and the degree of confidence inspired by Popular Unity's leadership.

Despite all this, the productive forces were not destroyed. On the contrary, Pedro Vuskovic reported that during 1972 "enterprises in the social sector have increased production by 15 percent." This was confirmed in a chart issued by SOFOFA (Sociedad de Fomento Fabril), the Chilean industrial bourgeoisie's employer association, which showed the percentage variation of production and sales of industrial products in the first eleven months of 1972 compared with the same period in 1971 when, let us recall, there had been a significant rise:

Table 5
Percent Change in Production and Sales Between
January and November 1972 and Corresponding Period 1971

	Production	Sales
Soft consumer goods	+0.5	+0.7
Durable consumer goods	−5.8	−6.0
Transport materials	+20.6	+1.8
Intermediate products for industry	+4.8	+6.0
Intermediate construction goods	+9.3	+5.2
Miscellaneous manufactured goods	+14.8	+13.4
Total industry	+4.0	+3.5

Source: *El Mercurio*, January 27, 1973.

In other words, the economic dislocation, the rising inflation which reached 163.4 percent in 1972, and the hoarding and speculation were the results of the class confrontation, of the popular masses' pressure for rapid improvement of their living standard, of the redistribution of income which was in large measure determined by the government's favoring of the workers, and also, of course, of the bourgeoisie's defensive response aiming to sharpen the political crisis—all of which was reflected in hoarding, speculation, and the black market. The economy was not destroyed; the workers were increasing production; the inefficiency of state-run enterprises was within bounds. The real explanation for the dislocation of various production and trade processes lay in the class struggle, which had moved massively on to this terrain.

Traditionally the Chilean state, through the Directorate of Industry and Trade, regulated the various sectors' interests, both between different strata of the bourgeoisie and in their economic relations with the rest of the population, by fixing prices of "prime necessities." This gave the executive a powerful weapon for determining income distribution. The government had responded to the workers' expectations by fixing prices of many articles of daily consumption—food, clothing, semi-durables—permitting new strata of the wage-earning population to buy more of them. In this situation the employers demanded as one of their basic claims "freedom of prices to put an end to the black market," a demand almost unconditionally defended by *El Mercurio* and the National and Christian Democratic parties.

At the end of 1972, as during the rest of the popular government period, distribution was effected through three channels: the traditional mechanism of established trade, the black market, and direct distribution.

To combat the black market, which in its last stage was largely carried on through establishments of the middle and small commercial bourgeoisie, the government had promoted the JAPs as associations of consumers, and finally these were given legal status by a resolution of February 3, 1972. But as the interior minister pointed out in 1973, ". . . the comptroller's office reviewing the resolution said that the JAPs' functions were merely to advise and cooperate with the public authority . . . and in short [the JAPs] lacked any executive or decision-making authority." In spite of this and of an *aide-mémoire* from General Prats, throughout Chile's cities the JAPs became a formidable weapon in the workers' fight against hoarding and speculation. It was mainly the women, directly affected by the supply problem, who got together in all the neighborhoods and *poblaciones* not only to compel merchants to sell the products they received, but to do so at official prices. A "denunciation" by the merchant organization SIDECO shows what happened: "After being forcibly removed from his house, each merchant found a queue of persons, brought by the same JAP members, lined up before his store . . . his stocks were sold at prices fixed by them, and even they could not explain how the prices were arrived at. . . . The actions of these JAPs did not stop until all the stocks he had for normal sale were sold out."[9]

Despite these adversities the bourgeoisie launched at the beginning of January an all-out campaign of hoarding, with the object of increasing shortages and thus assuring a bourgeois victory in the March 4, 1973, congressional elections.

Faced with the inadequacy of state mechanism, the government on January 10 created the National Distribution Secretariat to order and regulate wholesale and retail distribution, directing as follows: "On the basis of a per-family quota of necessities . . . of some thirty products, the people's organizations on the local level (JAPs, *comandos comunales*) in which merchants participate will program the periodic needs for essential products and determine the responsibilities of each local establishment with respect to their sale."[10] It was further laid down that all social-sector production would be channeled through state distributors; agricultural production in the land-reformed sector would also go through state channels, and there would be direct distribution—bypassing the merchants—to the lowest-income strata of the population, that is the inhabitants of *poblaciones* and *campamentos.*

The shot hit the target. The right wing reacted hysterically to a situation which was slipping from its control. On January 11 *El Mercurio* charged that "rationing destroys democratic guarantees" and, in a front-page article headed "The Threshold of Dictatorship," that the freedoms of opinion, expression, and assembly and the inviolability of the home were being threatened while "property rights with respect to commercial establishments and to merchandise in merchants' or private persons' possession become a dead letter with the plundering entry of the JAPs into merchandise distribution." In effect the spokesman of the bourgeoisie was defending the right to private property, and the right to hoard and speculate—in a word, the right to the highest rate of profit then obtainable in Chile—without regard for the people's essential needs, offering the bitter freedom of prices as sole alternative.

Despite waverings and retreats in their implementation, the measures taken did much to promote the countrywide spread of JAPs which fought the hoarders energetically and with positive results. The distribution battle would never be resolved; later, state distributors passed under control of the military, who gave merchants better guarantees, but JAP action evened the balance. In any case, this initiative had no small effect on the March 1973 election results.

From early November and the formation of the new cabinet, which attempted to provide a breathing space in the country's intense class struggle, the attention of both Popular Unity and opposition parties was focused on the upcoming elections. Consistent with the bounds of its strategy, the government had to seek new strength by constitutional means, that is, by a strong enough electoral showing to get the "dialogue" with Christian Democracy moving again under better conditions.

The opposition, for its part, had worked out various ways to halt the revolutionary process, ways reflecting not only the specific interests of sections of the bourgeoisie but the different stages of accumulation of forces which had supervened and combined in course of the process. Reaction had these options:

(1) The CIA-aided attempt at a military coup in October 1970 by retired General Viaux, which failed due to the existence of the "constitutionalist" sector in the armed forces and to the vigilance of the popular movement.

(2) The attempt to name Jorge Alessandri president (he had come in second in October 1970) with the object of opening the way to a new election in which all components of the bourgeoisie would be allied. This failed due to the refusal of a small but important Christian Democratic sector to go along—not to mention that at the time such a move would have involved violent confrontations which the ruling class wanted to avoid.

(3) Diversion of the popular government and its process into a reformist-populist trend which would halt the development of revolutionary consciousness and organization. This was frustrated in part by President Allende's convictions and by the radicalization of the workers, mainly expressed in the Socialist Party. The plan was put into operation under Christian Democratic guidance in the first months of 1971.

(4) Bringing about the government's overthrow or submission through "mass" bourgeois insurrection, as attempted by the reunited forces of reaction in October 1972. This had been defeated essentially

by the action of the workers and in part by the neutrality of the armed forces, which in that situation could not do otherwise.

(5) Removal of the president by Congress, a step constitutionally requiring a two-thirds vote. An option that the March 1973 elections might have made possible, defeated, however, by the workers' overwhelming electoral support of Popular Unity. All the opposition favored this.

(6) Forcing Allende's resignation, or calling a plebiscite which would open the way to his replacement—a plan proposed in the last months chiefly by Christian Democracy. Its failure was due to Allende's resoluteness, although on the day of the September 1973 coup he had a speech prepared announcing a plebiscite.

(7) A "white coup"—formation of an entirely military cabinet of which Allende would be a "constitutional" prisoner. This plan, also hatched by Christian Democracy, would have meant crushing the popular movement and was resisted by Allende, who fully understood its implications. Christian Democracy proposed it in the government's last days.

(8) A military coup as initially proposed by the employer guilds and by Patria y Libertad, later promoted by the National Party immediately after the March 1973 elections, and finally backed by Christian Democracy. This would succeed in September 1973.

(9) Civil war, considered as an alternative by the abovementioned organizations. It did not materialize due to the weak resistance the popular movement could offer to the coup d'état and to the dominant role of the conspirators in the military during the government's final months.

In March 1973 the unified Right hoped to win back the presidency by its "parliamentary" plan, by which it had to get 67 percent of the votes and two-thirds of the seats. The Christian Democrats shared in this aim, though with a shade of difference, as an optimal possibility and insisting that the elections should be considered as a plebiscite before which the government must bow.

To comprehend Christian Democracy's apparent vacillations and inconsistencies, one must remember that it had tried from the outset to present itself as an alternative to capitalism and socialism with a vague communitarian and Christian-social philosophy. During Frei's presidency his attempt to modernize the system of economic relations landed him in secondary contradictions with the old employer strata and with what remained of the agrarian oligarchy. At the same time the mass of Christian Democratic sympathizers contained broad popular sectors who in a distorted way made themselves felt in the party leadership. However, Frei had managed to maintain his leadership ever since 1958 when he appealed to the Liberal Party to support his presidential candidacy.

Thus, beyond the different options that it adopted in specific situations, Christian Democracy remained a defender of the capitalist system throughout its history, during which imperialism had never been shy about intervening on its behalf. It was not interested in destroying the state apparatus, but rather wanted to control it. At the same time it was not overly concerned when certain backward bourgeois sectors lost power, so long as the interests of the modern middle and big bourgeoisie were strengthened.

Nevertheless, as we have seen, whenever the government and the Communist Party sought a lasting understanding with Christian Democracy, based on policies which were largely the latter's, not only were no agreements reached but the talks were broken off and the Christian Democrats began wooing the National Party to join in strengthening the opposition.

The fact is that Christian Democracy lacked confidence, not in the intentions of those who pressed for "dialogue" with it, but in their capacity to slow down the process, to halt the radicalization of the popular movement by getting tough with the revolutionary Left, and to "consolidate" the situation. In the words of Renán Fuentealba, president of Christian Democracy and leader of its "progressive" wing: "The Christian Democratic Party calls upon Chileans to become fully aware of the significance of the antidemocratic threat posed by a government that is incapable of controlling economic and social processes, but at the same time is anxious to retain its present power and extend it drastically."[11]

So that although Christian Democracy deprecated the far-reaching policies of the government on various levels, and some of its sectors showed readiness to return—at any cost—to the situation prevailing before November 4, 1970, its main body was mainly concerned to constrict the workers' power of initiative; to eliminate the embryos of "popular power"—JAPs, *cordones industriales, comandos comunales*—by constant demands for the disarming of "parallel armies"; to alter the forms of workers' participation in the social sector; to return to a "normal" economy by freeing prices and suspending statifications; to subordinate the government to a Congress in which Christian Democracy would be determinant. In a word, it demanded that the popular government "control" the economic and social processes and so banish the specter of revolution.

Allende was not prepared to pay so high a price. His policy was to take two steps forward and one step back. Often he ended by taking one forward and two back, but he never accepted the ring of iron within which Christian Democracy wanted to confine the popular movement. His conception of the capture of power, and of the transformations undertaken, subordinated the support of the working class and workers to a paternalistic policy and limited their capacity for initiative but never ran counter to it. Allende sought to lead the popular movement in accordance with his ideas, but his convictions and background completely prevented him from setting himself against the movement and basing his government policy on opposition to it. That was just what the Christian Democrats demanded as the price of an agreement from mid-1972, when they shrewdly perceived that the revolutionary process had a potential that transcended the tactics that the Communist Party attempted to implement.

Christian Democracy aimed to win such broad support in March 1973 as would permit it to develop its policy within the institutional system, to confront the government with the backing of a substantial majority vote, including the two-thirds of the votes necessary for constitutional removal of President Allende.

Meanwhile other bourgeois sectors were getting set to enter a new phase. On February 22, Roberto Thieme, a leader of the fascistic Patria y Libertad with ties to big business and strong influence in the National Party, said: "The liberal democratic system dies for us on March 4. That is, there will be a plebiscite, many people will be fooled and will say that now there is no solution. But we say there is no political solution, we know the solution will not come through the traditional way of political parties. It will come by way of the armed forces and the working men."[12]

The march of events, proceeding on different levels, would finally put Christian Democracy out of the game on September 11, 1973. The class struggle was to destroy Chile's institutional system but not the capitalist state.

The hustings have never been the best ground for forces aiming to transform society. Ideology always lags behind changing material relations and thus becomes a superstructure that acts in defense of the established regime. The new, the unknown, is always feared. The present, although it does not satisfy individual aspirations, is what is real. At the same time, all material forces act in favor of maintaining the system and the media play a key role. The workers "have nothing to lose but their chains," but many popular strata, skilled workers, small campesinos, small businessmen, artisans fear for their modest interests, including their limited "social prestige" vis-à-vis more exploited sectors.

In September 1970 Popular Unity won 36.3 percent of the vote; in April 1971, with the bourgeoisie divided and disoriented, the euphoria produced by the first measures gave the government 50.5 percent. In March 1973 it got 43.4 percent—1,600,000 votes. And this with Congress, courts, and comptroller fiercely opposing all the executive's measures and blocking any wage-adjustment legislation; with hoarding and speculation raised to the levels of postwar Europe; with the opposition united around one central policy; with all the power of the big bourgeoisie who had brought into line all middle proprietors and most of the small propertied bourgeoisie. In short, with the whole might of traditionally dominant forces arrayed in furious battle against the Popular Unity parties.

The results surprised not only the opposition but also the left party leaders. The workers' response showed yet again the tremendous potential of a people disposed to open up the road of socialist transformations, regardless of obstacles and sacrifices implied in that commitment. The popular government had won a higher percentage of votes than any previous constitutional government after twenty-six months in office.

Yet there was no way to consolidate this victory within the institutional scheme followed by Popular Unity and the government. There was in fact no change in the relative composition of Congress: the opposition, with 54.5 percent, maintained its majority and could thus without additional difficulty continue the same systematic obstruction as before. And of course the relationship of forces with other state organs—courts, comptroller's office, armed forces—was modified even less.

In effect the working class was far from isolated: alongside it stood broad masses of campesinos, *pobladores,* white-collar state and private-enterprise employees, artisans, and to a smaller extent other strata of the population. But these could not make their weight effectively felt in state institutions. Furthermore, the government had to take into account the two great lines of the political spectrum which divided its base of support. On the one hand, the revolutionary Left saw this victory as the best evidence of the possibility of "advancing without compromise" and developing the organs of "popular power." On the other, the "institutional road" sector expected the solid electoral support expressed by the people to bring the talks with Christian Democracy finally to a successful conclusion, and to establish a long period of consolidation of transformations achieved within the constitutional framework. Thus the dominant sector of Popular Unity and the government had no alternative but to repeat the so-often-attempted line of alliance with the "middle classes." But electoral victories are only victories when a government is able to implement them, when the necessary means of enforcement exist, or when the opposition is not the dominant force in society. The only significance of Popular Unity's March 4, 1973, "electoral victory" within the bourgeois-democratic system was to show the tremendous popular support it enjoyed. And this made it the more dangerous.

The opposition's surprise did not last long. But at no time did it lose its composure. Within it, the sectors favoring a road other than the "parliamentary plan" immediately grew in influence. They had the great advantage of the initiative which the government delivered over to them. And they retained quite unimpaired all the power mechanisms they had used up to then. Constitutional removal of the president being beyond their power, they proceeded to develop the other alternatives.

Once again the popular government failed to grasp the opportunities which the workers' consciousness and energy offered it. The bourgeoisie would know how to exploit this weakness.

Table 6A

Electoral Evolution in Chile

	1969	*1970*	*1971*	*1973*
Popular Unity	889,490	1,011,209	1,431,357	1,589,025
	36.9%	36.3%	50.5%	43.4%
Christian	716,547	774,424	723,623	1,049,007
Democracy	29.8%	27.8%	25.6%	29.1%
National Party and	582,130	972,209	619,861	915,360
Radical Right*	24.2%	34.9%	22.0%	25.4%

*I have divided the 1969 Radical Party vote into the percentages that emerged in 1971 between the Radical Party and Radical Right, distributing them in that proportion between Popular Unity and the National Party.

Table 6B

	1967	*1969*	*1971*	*1973*
Communist Party	346,105	383,049	479,206	584,303
	14.8%	15.9%	17.0%	16.2%
Socialist Party	324,965	294,448	631,939	672,200
	13.9%	12.2%	22.4%	18.7%
Radical Party	377,074	313,559	225,851	134,008
	16.1%	13.0%	8.0%	3.7%
Christian	834,810	716,547	723,623	1,049,007
Democracy	35.6%	29.8%	25.6%	29.1%
National Party	334,656	480,523	511,669	767,663
	14.3%	20.0%	18.1%	21.3%
Radical Right	Included in Radical		108,192	147,697
	Party Column		3.8%	4.1%

1. *El Mercurio* (Santiago de Chile), January 25, 1973.
2. *El Mercurio*, January 27, 1973.
3. Carlos Altamirano, *Decisión Revolucionaria* (Santiago de Chile: Quimantú, 1973).
4. Resolution approved unanimously in the plenary of the Twenty-second General Congress of the Socialist Party.
5. Resolution approved by the Twenty-third General Congress of the Socialist Party at La Serena.
6. Altamirano, *Decisión Revolucionaria*.
7. *El Mercurio*, December 6, 1972.
8. *El Mercurio*, December 21, 1972.
9. *El Mercurio*, January 5, 1973. SIDECO is the Sindicato de Dueños de Establecimientos Comerciales.
10. *El Mercurio*, January 11, 1973.
11. *El Mercurio*, April 12, 1973.
12. *Chile Hoy* (Santiago de Chile), March 9, 1973.

8 THE INSTITUTIONS OF THE CAPITALIST STATE

The state is the aggregate of laws, institutions, and powers regulating a society in a given historical context. The Popular Unity government's program stated: "Chile is a capitalist country, dependent on imperialism, dominated by sectors of the bourgeoisie which are structurally linked to foreign capital, and which cannot resolve the country's basic problems because these arise precisely from their own class privileges which they will never voluntarily renounce." Thus in 1970 the Chilean state was the superstructural expression of the regulation of a bourgeois-dominated capitalist society. This hegemony meant that Chile's laws and institutions were created precisely to suppress the resistance of the exploited classes as well as to set firm foundations for and strengthen the dominant class's economic, social, and political power. That is, the state was organized as a function of class interests.

It should be added that the state was not a simple arithmetical sum of the various institutions and powers composing it, but a coherent and complementary totality of those institutions and powers, expressing the values of the prevailing capitalist system.

Chile's state institutions were based on the 1925 Constitution which established close interdependence among the three classic powers of capitalist democracies: executive, legislative, judicial. Precisely because of the close ties among those powers, the various bourgeois strata—financial, industrial, agrarian, and commercial—had to keep seeking convergence between differing propertied interests. In 1925 the Chilean bourgeoisie provided themselves with a sufficiently malleable' and elastic mechanism of government to ensure that competition to manage the country would never imperil the really fundamental interests of any capitalist stratum, despite the constant frictions.

The Chilean state in 1970 was a complex mechanism with diverse components. Due to the harmonious and complementary functioning of all of these, the mechanism directed and organized society for the ruling class's benefit, exploiting workers and other propertyless classes through a "representative democracy" under which president and Congress were elected by universal and secret ballot. Other not-to-be-omitted components of the state mechanism—basic ones in view of their authority and functions—were the comptroller's office and the armed forces.

We should recall again here that Chile's relatively early industrialization produced a high level of consciousness and organization among the workers, whose struggles resulted in various gains of a democratic character. While these gains never changed or endangered the prevailing social system, after 1933 they did open the way for expression of immediate mass interests through popular participation in state institutions.

These institutions were not static organisms isolated from society but quite the reverse: in their deformations, their retreats, and their advances they expressed the various stages of the class struggle in Chile.

We must also note that just because the state apparatus was so solid, and the various propertied strata so skilled in finding areas of agreement to manage the country and dominate society, after 1933 the need did not arise to call on the armed forces save at occasional critical moments; thus, in contrast to the rest of Latin America, the military played no major role in Chile over a long period. From which arises the myth of their professionalism and of the Chilean state's capacity to rule without their aid.

The institutions of the capitalist state were decisively involved in developing the society with all its contradictions; but four decades of "peaceful" evolution had created an image of increasing proficiency, feeding the widespread illusion that, as evolution flowed on, those institutions could be harnessed to the service of revolutionary changes. Leaders and parties professing a scientific socialist conception of Chilean society postulated a gradual transfer of economic, social, and political power from the bourgeois class to an alliance dominated by the proletariat. Hence their belief that the various state organs would continue functioning harmoniously and would be progressively subjected to working-class will, graciously accepting their own replacement and demise. But let us see how these institutions performed during the Popular Unity government, that is, in a period of intense class struggle when the model of capitalist domination was challenged.

Within the balance and inter-relation of powers laid down by the 1925 Constitution, the president of the Republic had broad functions: appointment of state ministers, top officials in all public agencies, ambassadors, commissioners, and governors; supervision of the treasury and investment of state income according to law; establishment of prices for "basic necessities"; adjustment of wages for state and private-enterprise workers; execution of all laws passed by Congress; and disposition of the armed forces which were under his authority.

The legislative power was bicameral: a chamber of deputies with 150 members, a senate with 50. The electoral system divided the country into thirty-one districts which elected one deputy for every 30,000 electors and every fraction exceeding 15,000. Senators were elected on the basis of ten provincial groupings. The right to vote extended to all citizens, literate or illiterate, who were over 18 and inscribed in electoral registers open the year round. The ballot was secret, with various provisions to eliminate bribery, and so broad that in 1973, out of a population of less than ten million, 3,355,000 persons went to the polls.

The legislative power's authority included its mandatory approval of all laws proposed by the president. The senate, at the request of the chamber of deputies, could decide by simple majority to remove state ministers or by two-thirds vote to remove the president. The national Congress had authority to approve or reject the budget submitted by the executive. The Congress could reject any presidential bill by simple majority, but a two-thirds vote was necessary to override the president on bills originating in either chamber.

Clearly visible in all these provisions were the extent to which the two powers were interdependent and the need for their complementary action to assure a harmonious course for the nation. The constitutional clash in Chile developed over a long period precisely because Popular Unity controlled the presidency and more than a third of Congress. The opposition could not impose its will for lack of the necessary two-thirds, but it did have more than half, enough to hobble or halt all of the executive power's legislative initiatives.

The judicial power enjoyed great independence, including authority to appoint its own officials in a strictly hierarchical order, and to use the law enforcement agencies to execute decisions it had reached on the basis of an extraordinarily antiquated and class-warped body of laws. The whole structure of the courts was steeped in a reactionary spirit which, due to their complete autonomy, was quite immune to any popular expression. Not only did the laws reflect the class system, but the judges dispelled any doubt of that fact in their interpretations.

The comptroller's office was an institution with the attributes of a fourth state power. It had review authority over the administration to decide whether or not the executive was acting constitutionally. Thus the executive's decrees, orders, and resolutions could not be implemented until the comptroller declared them legal. And note that both the comptrollership and the Supreme Court presidency were lifetime positions.

The first institution to react in defense of the capitalist system and of what is most essential to it—ownership of the means of production—was the comptroller's office. The government proceeded to apply a decree already in force—No. 520—permitting any industry with labor conflicts to be intervened and become a candidate for the social sector: a procedure which curtailed bourgeois power and developed a planned economic model based on state intervention. But in mid-1971 the comptroller's office began rejecting executive decrees based on this interpretation of the laws: "The comptroller's office considers itself juridically compelled to advise you that it is not possible, in law, to uphold the validity of the resolutions." The resolutions in question referred to the intervention of Manufacturas Sumar, Paños Oveja Tomé, Lanera Austral, Algodones Hirmas, Rayonhil, and Yarur SA—that is, the nucleus of the textile monopoly. Under the law the executive's problem could be resolved by a "decree of insistence" to which the comptroller must submit, but such a decree required a completely homogeneous cabinet: all of its members must sign.

The comptroller's office continued this line of action but toughened it early in 1973, rejecting numerous government decrees. Since the government then contained three military ministers, it did not insist. Also rejected by the comptroller was a decree to democratize education; and previously that office had busied itself with limiting the authority of such government-created organs as the campesino councils and JAPs, on the ground that executive decrees could only confer advisory functions and that a law—i.e., parliamentary approval—was necessary to confer executive ones. In March 1973 the comptroller's office challenged the conduct of a governmental agency, stating that "neither the political constitution, nor any law, grants to the minister of economy or any other minister the power to review actions of the comptroller general."

The first big clash between executive and Congress came when the latter approved by simple majority a constitutional-reform bill defining the three areas of the economy, which in substance gave the opposition majority the say on what enterprises could be taken into the social sector. Thus Congress emerged clearly as the defender of the monopolist bourgeoisie's interests and property, and an attempt was made to take back part of the power which was constitutionally out of its hands. In July 1972 Congress overrode by simple majority the executive veto of this bill, in open breach of the Constitution; the government reacted by announcing it would submit the controversy to the constitutional tribunal created by the Statute of Guarantees in 1970. Also early in 1972 Congress approved the first impeachment charges against a minister of state, forcing the government to dismiss the minister and warning it that all parliamentary mechanisms within the law would be used to oppose the government's policy.

Meanwhile the judicial power was also moving ahead to block the executive's freedom of action, by upholding measures taken by the other powers to maintain capitalism. Thus *El Mercurio* reported on January 5, 1972: "The courts restored the Talca newspaper *La Mañana* to its owner, after a strike in which the building was occupied for more than four months. The striking workers engaged in all kinds of maneuvers to get the government to intervene, but without success." Actually, the frank *El Mercurio* news report confirmed the class motivation of the judicial power, as well as the limitations that prevailing capitalist laws imposed on the executive. *El Mercurio* proclaimed with visible satisfaction on the same day: "The Supreme Court, by considering the appeal of Manufacturas de Algodón Yarur, SA, has opened the road for the petitioner to appeal the Directorate of Industry and Trade's order requisitioning the factory." Thus Chile's

powerful textile monopoly found its natural defender in state
institutions.

By the end of 1972 the machinery for regulating society showed
clear signs of stalling. The appeals court named a minister to try a case
against a cabinet member, the comptroller's office declared the
government's actions illegal, and the chamber of deputies approved a
bill in which it was stated: "The government has consistently and
repeatedly violated constitutional provisions, and done so in matters so
fundamental to a democracy as freedom of expression, which places
said government outside the law."[1]

Thus Congress, courts, and comptroller intensified their concerted
onslaught against a government whose program called for total
adherence to legality—a legality which was of bourgeois-democratic
vintage and which furthermore, due to the government's vacillations,
could now no longer be modified. In February 1973 the power to
obstruct executive actions was shown even more clearly by Congress,
which by rejecting the government's wage- and salary-adjustment bill
hoped to provoke reaction by the workers (now showing signs of
anxiety) and also to influence the elections due in March.

In fact the executive power was by then no longer the dynamic
center of the state, for the opposition forces defending capitalist
continuity found in the powers they controlled the necessary and
sufficient mechanism to block all government initiatives. The judicial
power and the comptroller interpreted the prevailing laws and moni-
tored their application, and new laws could not be approved without
the assent of Christian Democracy in Congress.

The balance and indispensable complementariness of powers were
preventing the regulation of society, and the institutional well showed
signs of running dry. At the same time the government held fast to the
thesis of Allende and the Communist Party that it derived its main
authority from the legitimacy of its origin and the legality of its
actions. So that even as it confronted the bourgeois roadblock within
the institutional system, it was at pains to subdue and discipline the
popular movement with such rebukes as this by the interior minister:
"The government is sure that [these] irresponsible attitudes do not
reflect the real feeling of workers and *pobladores,* who in their great majority reject these procedures and support the plans of the authorities. . . .
The government will be inflexible in the observance of prevailing laws
for maintaining public order."[2]

By then a whole sector of the Left understood that class antagonisms could not be resolved within capitalist institutionality. A "Political Document" of the Socialist Party's Santiago regional district said:

> Every state sector of which we can take control is important, so long as we don't lose sight of our central objective, which is liquidation of the bourgeois state. That enormous bureaucratic machine is useless in every way for the construction of socialism. One can't talk of building socialism without taking power, and that in turn implies destruction of the bourgeois state and construction of a new one—a workers' socialist state which will begin withering away as the building of socialism proceeds. . . . We have reached the point in this country where no substantial advance is possible without a definition as to who is in charge. . . . Up to now Chilean workers have more and more demonstrated their capacity for discipline and for taking the offensive. Only the vacillations, indecisions, and waverings of the top echelons have prevented greater advances. Those same workers will lose heart if their strength is not effectively used against the Right, or is merely used as a form of pressure for later negotiation.[3]

The March 1973 elections were far from resolving the conflict of state powers, since they left unchanged the proportional relation in Congress between Popular Unity and the opposition. They only intensified the friction between the various powers. On May 11 President Allende said in a speech to the nation:

> Yesterday I called for the intervention of the Constitutional Tribunal. I did so to request a ruling on the way Congress had dealt with my vetoes of the bill modifying the Fundamental Law. This bill obstructs formation of the social sector and consolidates the capitalist regime. The procedure followed by the present majority in both chambers represents a grave threat to the very essence of our institutional system.[4]

The response was not long in coming. On May 1 Senate President Frei and Chamber of Deputies President Pareto—another Christian Democrat—sent to the comptroller's office the bill approved by the reactionary majority in both chambers. "The only duty of the president of the Republic," they said, "is to comply with Article 109 of the state political constitution, which stipulates that if the executive does not call a plebiscite within the constitutional time limit, the bill approved by Congress becomes law."[5]

The judiciary also stepped up its criticism, the Supreme Court thus addressing the president on May 17:

> The surrogate judge of Melipilla, don Mario González, has reported that in the case of land usurpation at the "Las Rosas" estate the Melipilla *carabineros* were ordered to evict the invaders of said property, but that as in previous and similar cases the chief of the *carabineros,* don Sergio Silva, did not carry out said order but returned it to the court, stating that he did so by instruction of the commissioner in Santiago.[6]

Defense of landowners was among the characteristic concerns of the judicial power, which from the Supreme Court president down to the base of its hierarchical pyramid was manned precisely by big landowners or members of their families. The government, no matter how anxious to act within strict legality, could hardly use the repressive apparatus against the campesino movement without denying its very self, and hence avoided such requirements by using its constitutional authority over the *carabineros* and other armed bodies.

A further step in questioning the government's legality was taken at the end of that month when the Supreme Court addressed the executive as follows:

> . . . . the obstruction of the *carabineros* in carrying out the orders of a criminal court, which under law must be executed by said body without any obstacle, . . . signifies an open persistence in rebellion against judicial decisions, in disregard of the alteration produced in the judicial order by such alterations and omissions, and further signifies not merely a crisis in the state of law as was represented to Your Excellency in the previous communication, but a peremptory or imminent breakdown of the rule of law in the country.[7]

The government's reaction could not have been more defensive. President Allende replied to the Supreme Court: "It is consequently inadmissible to maintain that these authorities must lend absolutely indiscriminate police protection, since this could lead to situations that would specifically threaten the social peace and public order which they are called upon to preserve."[8] In this way the Allende administration continued to refuse to challenge the behavior and the provocations of the judiciary, one of the most reactionary of all the Chilean governmental bodies, but rather implicitly conferred authority on it by accepting the discussion along the lines formulated by the Supreme Court.

After the conflict between the executive and Congress had been submitted to the Constitutional Tribunal, and the tribunal declared itself incompetent, the last interior minister said: "Acceptance of the Congress's thesis would mean ending the presidential system and falling into the pernicious regime of pseudoparliamentarianism. . . . The comptroller's office, in a surprising opinion, has attributed to itself powers that it does not constitutionally possess. . . ."[9]

The truth is that capture of the executive power by the workers' parties had resulted in profound dislocation of the whole institutional machinery. It had reduced the bourgeoisie's capacity for action on the economic level by preventing its normal accumulation of surplus value and, even more importantly, had cut off its access to state repressive bodies, with the consequence that struggles for popular demands gathered strength and new forms of worker and campesino organization emerged. At the end of May, however, the institutional system also showed that, far from having become independent of the social classes that created and perfected it, it was adapting itself to new circumstances so as to block the whole process of change, and was leading Chile into a situation from which there was no "legal," "peaceful," or "institutional" exit other than restoring executive power to the bourgeoisie.

Champions of the Constitution kept multiplying their appeals to the armed forces, thus showing their true function as servants of a social class, and the opposition parties renewed their demands:

> Once again the nation's institutionality has broken down in consequence of the "takeovers" of manufacturing establishments. . . . It is a matter of extreme gravity that the president of the Republic has given his support to the organizers of these outrages. . . . This situation, incompatible with our democratic and republican regime, makes it necessary for the armed forces to enforce the Arms Control Law in order to avoid the formation of an extremist army. . . .[10]

The appeal would not fall on deaf ears.

On August 22, 1973, the National and Christian Democratic majority in the Chamber of Deputies put through a resolution which the right wing called "historic." "The government," it said, "has not violated the Constitution and the law in isolated instances only but has made these violations a permanent system of conduct." It called on the armed forces to repudiate government policy and said that otherwise the presence of military ministers in the cabinet would seriously compromise the armed forces' professional character "by open violation of Article 22 of the political Constitution, gravely endangering their institutional prestige." [11]

Thus a cycle had come to an end. Chile's institutional system had clearly shown its class character, and in the face of the impossibility of loosening the shackles that had been placed on it, the ruling classes did not hesitate to use the very state institutions they controlled to break it, in order that the capitalist system should be maintained, the popular movement suppressed, and a "normal" economy restored which would guarantee surplus value and the security of their property. From then on the regulator of Chilean society would be another state agency: the armed forces.

After the fall of General Ibáñez's dictatorship in 1931 the Chilean state had passed through various stages which expressed the commitment and interrelationships of various classes and social strata. From 1938 on, there had been a series of governments with Communist and Socialist participation, which helped to stabilize the institutional system by bringing parties representative of the workers' immediate interests into the responsibilities of administering capitalist society. This recognition of the exploited classes' weight in regulating society was an advance; yet the great limitations on their participation, within a system of bourgeois economic, social, and political supremacy, must be appreciated. Development of the democratic model of domination was interrupted in 1948 when the industrial bourgeoisie deemed it necessary to subdue and paralyze labor-union struggles with the "Law of Defense of Democracy," which outlawed the Communist Party and persecuted the whole popular movement. From 1953 a series of events made new relationships of forces possible: the workers managed to create a front of parties independent of the bourgeoisie and a union confederation which improved their negotiating position. Although bourgeois interests predominated in the state as a whole, there was a progressive democratization through the electoral law, the labor code, and the institutionalized participation of workers' parties in the legislative power. Finally, with the split in the bourgeoisie caused by its two different development models, Chile reached the 1970 presidential elections as an advanced democratic state, in which the delicate balance of its components showed the precariousness of capitalist preponderance and the maturing of working-class consciousness, organization, and ability to run the country. In other words, a period then began in which the traditional system of domination faced a serious challenge.

The popular government put into practice a policy which reflected the idealization of democracy as something outside the class-struggle dialectic, and which envisaged the possibility of separating the state apparatus created by Chilean society under bourgeois rule from the material and political interests that forged the apparatus. The solid historical fact is that during the Popular Unity government the body of institutions forming the Chilean state lost the coherence and harmony that had previously allowed it to run the country. This produced a conflict of constitutional powers which reflected the drastic sharpening of the class struggle. What was at issue was the management of society by one of the two basic classes comprising it, proletariat and bourgeoisie. In the March 1973 elections the bourgeoisie had its last chance to unify the state institutions under its hegemony, by winning two-thirds of the congressional seats and thus recovering those constitutional mechanisms which would permit it to subordinate the executive power. Having seen these hopes dashed through the extraordinary vote rolled up by Popular Unity, the bourgeois opposition, both political party and "guild," moved directly on to the road of subverting legality as an immediate objective.

In the face of this the government criticized the institutions that served the reactionary opposition, but even when those institutions exceeded the limits of their legal authority it never questioned their existence. That is, Popular Unity's criticism was purely verbal and did not proceed into the realm of action, of presenting an active and coherent proposal for their replacement. Hence, too, it always had to insist on subordination of the workers to prevailing legality—capitalist legality—to the detriment of the new popular power models of organization.

To sum up, the rise of workers' parties within the institutional regime through the presidency of the Republic meant:

(1) A substantial part of the material assets under state administration came under control of the left parties and helped develop the popular organizations.

(2) Until July 1973, the subordination of the state repressive apparatus to the executive power resulted in its nonuse against the city and rural workers' struggles, enabling these to grow in strength to the detriment of the owners, who were powerless to use it in the traditional manner.

(3) A substantial redistribution of national income in favor of wage-earners, and the formation of a Social Production Sector, highly significant in the national economy and taken from the bourgeoisie's hands, resulted in the complete dislocation of the capitalist system and the weakening of the bourgeoisie's capacity for action.

(4) The institutional mechanisms controlled by the executive power did not at any stage suffice—despite the repeated efforts of the government and a sector of Popular Unity—to "consolidate" the process and stabilize interclass economic and political relations.

(5) The mass movement found itself confined within the bourgeois-democratic legal system, with all the limitations that that involved, the system acting mainly as a brake on the development and strengthening of popular-power organizations aiming at a new form of state management.

(6) Chile's institutional system showed itself to be tightly linked with the interests of the class that had created and perfected it, and hence quite inadequate to assure progress toward socialism and bring the workers to the helm of society.

The heart of state power is the capacity to dispose of property and of the armed forces. We have already seen how the bourgeoisie found the necessary mechanisms to block the government's and the workers' advance toward control of ownership of the means of production and management of the national economy. Now let us see what happened with the armed forces.

The Chilean army was born with independence from Spain and was closely tied from the outset to the structures of the young state. Its history throughout the past century had been linked to the clashes between different owning groups, the most noteworthy being the civil war of 1891 when Adm. Jorge Montt defeated the constitutionalist forces of President José Manuel Balmaceda, which closed the cycle of liberal governments and opened an era of parliamentarianism. Between

1924 and 1932 the army played a decisive role by means of coups d'état of highly heterogeneous types, ushering in a variety of tendencies in a period when the army was split into factions which had trouble achieving stability under the Constitution approved in 1925. Another constant characteristic apart from this close dependency on state structures was that the army took full responsibility for whatever violence was required to hold the workers down. The massacres of workers in the Santa María de Iquique nitrate fields (1907), in San Gregorio (1921), La Coruña (1925), the cities of Vallenar and Copiapó (1931), the capital Santiago (April 2, 1957), the *población* Caro (1962), the El Salvador mines (1968), and finally the city of Puerto Montt in 1969, were all expressions of the armed forces' function, in service to the capitalist state, of suppressing workers' rebellions against exploitation.

Owing, as we have noted, to the development of Chile's institutions, to the different propertied strata's capacity for finding common policy ground as a class, and to the integration of workers' parties into the system, the military did not play a dominant role after 1933. But groups within the armed forces—under Gen. Ariosto Herrera in 1939, Ramón Vergara in 1948, twice during the Ibáñez constitutional regime (1952–1958), and under General Viaux in 1969—repeatedly tried to gain control of the state in situations where the civic institutions seemed weak or at least needed coercive force to subdue heightened popular insurgency.

Thus by 1970 the armed forces showed two outstanding traits: their dependence on state institutions (giving rise to the confusion about their "professionalism") and, closely akin to this, their tradition as suppressors of any and all popular rebellion.

To round out the picture with the social background of the armed forces' top men, a study in 1967 showed the following class composition of War Academy and Polytechnic School graduates: upper, 29 percent; middle, 65 percent, lower middle, 6 percent. The parents of thirty-seven generals who retired between 1952 and 1964 were: entrepreneurs, 22 percent; professionals and managers, 51 percent; farmers, 19 percent; white-collar employees, 8 percent. The military interviewees listed these as the occupations of their five closest civilian friends: managers and professionals, 86.1 percent; landowners, 8.3 percent; politicians, 2.8 percent; entrepreneurs, 2.8 percent; white-collar employees, none; workers, none.[12]

The stated purpose of Chile's armed institutions was defense of national security—a dynamic concept of protecting territorial integrity against any foreign aggressor to which, by way of ideological additive, the "cold war" tacked on defense of "republican and democratic" institutions against the internal enemy. That is from that time the Chilean military incorporated into its ideology a fierce anticommunism based on the U.S.'s global antagonism to the USSR, which included maintenance of capitalism as part of its mission. Their ideology was deeply impregnated with the concepts of hierarchy, discipline, authority, and order, and their ideal image of how a society should function developed and progressed on the basis of those elements, in a mechanical transference of its own table of organization to the state as a whole.

From the signing of the Inter-American Mutual Assistance Treaty in 1947, relations between the Chilean armed forces and their U.S. confrères were extremely close. Most of Chile's military superstructure consisted of materiel, techniques, and training supplied by the United States, and this was reinforced by the Military Assistance Pact which modernized all its equipment and gave Chile more military "aid" than any other Latin American country except Brazil. This state of affairs was never called into question during the popular government. At a time when Chile's economy was blocked by the actions of various public and private U.S. agencies, both military loans and the training of Chilean officers in the Canal Zone and within the United States continued without interruption. Many of the top officers who were subsequently to organize the coup d'état had been graduates of the "U.S. Army School of the Americas" in the Zone, and the four members of the junta of September 11, 1973, had received military and ideological training in the United States and in the Zone school.[13] Also the U.S. and Chilean fleets carried out joint maneuvers during the popular government's three years, the so-called "Unitas" operations to integrate strategy against the "common enemy." The U.S. armed forces' material, technical, and ideological presence in their relations with their Chilean counterparts had an impact that was never properly assessed, much less challenged. It reflected the strategic lines of the 1969 Rockefeller Report which in substance recommended that U.S. aid be granted to specified Latin American military regimes.

We must also note how the international situation in Latin America's Southern Cone affected the armed institutions. In Peru, beginning in 1968, a "progressive" military government was reorganizing society on the basis of a confluence of different capitalist tendencies with a shared view of the state as developer of the productive forces—a potential danger to the Chilean bourgeoisie's aspirations in the Andean market. Gen. Juan José Torres's government in Bolivia was overthrown in 1971 and replaced by the new military figure, Col. Hugo Banzer, apparently linked with the expansionist ambitions of the so-called "Brazilian sub-imperialism" which was gradually extending its role in Latin America under a military dictatorship installed in 1964. In Argentina Juan D. Perón finally returned to the helm following a compromise with that country's armed forces, which had been decisive in its politics since the early 1940s. In Uruguay the armed forces had been the manifest power behind the throne since 1972. Thus by 1973 the armed forces were clearly preponderant in all the Southern Cone countries bordering on or close to Chile.

Article 22 of Chile's political Constitution set forth that "the public force consists solely and exclusively of the armed forces and the *carabineros* which are essentially professional, hierarchical, disciplined, and nondeliberative institutions." This actually corresponded with reality at the outset of the popular government, when the armed forces were responsive to the executive power's constitutional authority—a situation also, however, reflecting the weakness of military reactionaries after the abortive October 1970 coup to prevent Salvador Allende from becoming president.

Popular Unity's policy toward the armed forces sought to keep them in submission to the government during the transformation process, hoping to achieve this by bringing them into the process. That is, their "professional" character, plus the institutional legality of the socioeconomic measures taken, plus the class alliance that was to be forged, were pillars of an overall policy which, it was expected, would evoke progressively less military resistance while at the same time giving the armed forces a new content to strengthen their "patriotic and constitutionalist" elements. Fundamental to the government's analysis were the armed forces' apparently strong links to and dependency on the state, and the social background and ties of top officers who identified themselves with the "middle classes."

And for a time this policy seemed to be viable. For as we have seen, military reactionaries failed to develop resistance during the government's first twenty-four months, and during the bourgeois insurrection of October 1972 the armed forces still maintained discipline and obedience to the executive power.

In fact, however, they divided early on—even before November 4, 1970—into two factions. One of these sectors, the "constitutionalists," represented first by General Schneider and after his assassination by General Prats, was of a reformist bent and sought moderate implementation of a policy of changes which would not endanger "social peace" and "national security." This sector's position was clearly set forth in Carlos Prats's statements and in the attitudes of other military members who joined the cabinet on November 3, 1972.

The other sector, the "institutionalists," reflected a much more clearly defined reactionary line. It deeply distrusted the government's ideologies, tactics, and strategies, was particularly apprehensive of the Communist Party's participation in it, and saw its own role in state institutions not as submission to the executive power but as maintenance of the economic and social status quo.

On October 21, 1972, the Arms Control Law, No. 17,798, was promulgated. It was based on a government draft to which the opposition, especially the Christian Democrats, had appended numerous clauses totally separating the armed forces from executive control in the matter of authority to investigate, house-search, keep under surveillance, and arrest anyone accused of possessing arms of any description. Technical errors never fully explained prevented the executive from using its constitutional prerogative to veto the opposition's amendments, and thus a legal weapon was surrendered of which the military reactionaries would later make full use.

In the last months of 1972 several significant events occurred. The military "constitutionalists" under Carlos Prats joined the cabinet to assure "social peace," a development thus interpreted by Socialist Minister of Agriculture Rolando Calderón: "The armed forces . . . enter the cabinet to preserve an institutional system which the hottest heads in the opposition wish to destroy. In this way they help assure the conditions for the program to advance." [14]

An *El Mercurio* editorial interpreted the presence of the military in the cabinet with more profundity, but with the same emphasis on the institutional system:

> The role they [the armed forces] have assumed since the October stoppage has been neither desired nor brought about by the high command. It has arisen as a consequence of the failure of the Popular Unity government's political cadres to maintain minimal

conditions of national security. . . . The Marxists' anxiety about the major role now being played by the armed forces is very understandable. While the military will not lend themselves to the political objectives of the opposition parties, and do not desire a sort of restoration of past economic rights and situations, they are certainly not disposed to let this country disintegrate as a national entity.[15]

During the same period, resolutions of a Socialist Party plenum included this: "Participation of members of the armed forces has helped to head off the maneuvers of a bourgeois and imperialist counter-revolution which, with its fascist demonstrations, has never stopped seeking to unleash civil war to put an end to the popular government." The Communist Party agreed with this appraisal, describing the armed forces' presence in the government as "highly positive for the country. . . . One must bear in mind . . . the stability the government has achieved with the three military ministers."[16] In truth both statements covered only part of the process that was complemented by the analysis of *El Mercurio*. Later events would show that the armed forces' participation in the government achieved neither "social peace" nor the hoped-for class alliance. If the Prats-Millas cabinet did stabilize the government during its five months in office, it also markedly weakened the dynamic of the popular movement's organization of new structures. At the same time it helped to weaken the "constitutionalist" sector of the armed forces, which was powerless to halt the polarization of Chilean society.

Another important event occurred in December 1972. The judicial power agreed to reduce to "two years second-degree imprisonment the sentence imposed on the felon Roberto Viaux as author of the crime of simple kidnapping of General Schneider."[17] Thus one state institution clearly showed its colors and objectives by an incredible decision lowering to two years the sentence on the assassin of the armed forces' commander-in-chief, and showed its open collusion with the military "institutionalists" (that is, reactionaries) who, clearly in response to the sharpened class struggle in the country, were beginning to reveal themselves openly. Signs of a split within the armed forces were plainly visible at the end of December and General Prats confessed his fears when he said: "Civil war . . . would plunge the country into chaos from which it would not recover in fifty years."[18]

The effect of the Prats cabinet's failure would be to intensify the contradictions within the armed forces and the reactionary and fascistic tendencies which the bourgeoisie skillfully stimulated. Immediately after the March elections the president of the chief employers' association, COPCOM (Production and Trade Confederation), said:

It is the duty of three basic forces to assume a decisive role in the new political and social organization. These are: parties which are disposed to build and not provoke chaos, the armed forces whose action is indispensable to restore discipline and efficiency and progress, and the employer guilds which constitute the lever of development and the cohesive factor of the national community.[19]

To this the "constitutionalists," now considerably weakened, replied through Prats: "Those who slander and insult the commander-in-chief in hope of tarnishing his professional prestige and weakening his authority in order to divide the officer corps from the High Command make the same mistake as those who would drive a wedge between officers and NCOs to make the institution break down."[20]

But the one who made an incorrect evaluation was General Prats. By May the reactionary sectors had gathered considerable strength and Col. Cristián Ackerknecht ordered a raid on the Socialist Party headquarters in the city of Rancagua following a confrontation between party members and fascist bands. The colonel's action had the support of the army's acting commander-in-chief, Gen. Augusto Pinochet.

In the same period the Retired Generals and Admirals Corps issued an openly subversive declaration revealing the imminence, extent, and motives of the putschist action: "It is startling to observe how the public force has lost its authority to impose order . . . disappointing to see the meager results of the application of the Arms Control Law and the notoriously partisan way it has been applied." The declaration added ominously: "If the Constitution is arbitrarily interpreted or is not respected, actions arising therefrom would be illegal, and this would justify cutting the present connection between the authorities and the armed forces."[21]

June 29 brought the mutiny of the 2nd Armored Regiment under Colonel Roberto Souper Onfray, which was suppressed by various units under Prats's direct command. The "constitutionalists" were still not strong enough to provoke civil war, hence massive participation by the putschist elements was not forthcoming. But the government, quite incapable of generating its own policies vis-à-vis the armed forces, left investigation and punishment of the authors of the coup to the discretion of the internal military services, as if this whole situation had no political content. Far from being used to purge the putschist officers with support of the "constitutionalist" sector, the defeat of the June 29 *tancazo* became a signal for reactionary escalation on every level of the state apparatus and especially in the armed forces.

The state institutions' reply to the abortive coup was total silence. For the Chamber of Deputies and Senate, the Supreme Court, and the comptroller general—all such zealous defenders of the Constitution when it was a matter of criticizing the government and the popular movement—it was inopportune to mention the attempted sedition, as though it had never occurred. Once again the institutions displayed their class character, and opposition deputies spurned the government's appeal to declare a state of siege.

Early in July the three branches of the military launched an all-out campaign of raiding factories, union offices, campuses, and even Left party headquarters, leaving a trail of dead, wounded, and imprisoned across the land. The object of this was twofold. The first and most obvious aim, concealed behind the Arms Control Law, was to learn the effective military capacity of the workers and to intimidate them by the regular forces' deployment of firepower. That military objective was fully achieved: "parallel armies" were found to be nonexistent, while workers and their leaders saw how ineffective their organization was against the armed forces' operational capacity.

The second objective, also military but internal, was to measure the strength of "constitutionalist" elements among officers and NCOs, with necessary "adjustments" in view. The operation, consisting of twenty-three raids between July 2 and August 3 alone, was a complete success for the preparation of the putschist maneuvers which won the opposition parties' applause.

But the abortive June 29 coup had also evoked general discussion within all branches of the armed forces; and while the "institutionalists" were decisively gaining ground among officers, there was a marked reaction among NCOs against the fascistic harangues. This was dealt with in the navy by arresting and torturing men who expressed loyalty to the government. When the navy high command accused Socialist Party, MAPU, and MIR general secretaries Altamirano, Garretón, and Enríquez of the crime of "incitement to subversion," the government not only failed to defend and support the tortured sailor-suspects but, in a new display of weakness and legalistic folly, denounced the "attempts by ultra-Left sectors to organize cells in ships of the national fleet." The movement of resistance against the putschist officers was strangled at birth, for clearly the lack of executive support made its growth impossible.

Penetration of the armed forces to try to develop tendencies favorable to its position was from the outset a preoccupation of the MIR, but its success was very limited. In mid-July it stepped up its propaganda, calling on NCOs and troops to demand "voting rights, promotion from the ranks, and the rights to assemble freely, receive fair pay, participate in people's organizations, and disobey officers who incited to coup d'état." And Altamirano thus addressed members of the armed forces:

> Soldiers, sailors, airmen, and *carabineros* cannot at any time or under any circumstances stoop to murder workers. More plainly still, it is their duty not only to ignore orders that involve shooting against the people or taking part in putschist adventures against the workers' government, but actively to oppose such orders. We are confident that this patriotic, national, and revolutionary criterion will prevail over the bourgeoisie's desperate maneuvers.[22]

In truth the bourgeoisie was far from desperate; on the contrary, it had succeeded by then in totally altering in its own favor the relation of forces between "constitutionalists" and "institutionalists," and was energetically preparing to sweep the government off the stage. The principal reasons for the strengthening of reactionaries and weakening of reformists in the armed forces were the polarization of society, the bourgeoisie's demand that popular parties be ousted from the public administration, the rise of the labor movement and its new organic expressions, the failure of the economic program, and the predominance of reaction in the ideological contest.

On August 22, Generals Mario Sepúlveda and Guillermo Pickering resigned, due to their loss of command authority and in veiled criticism of the government's incredible passivity. On August 23, army commander-in-chief General Prats tendered his irrevocable resignation. The departure of the three meant total defeat for the military "constitutionalists." Events moved fast and a few days later one of the dependent organs of the state apparatus smashed all prevailing institutionality to safeguard what was fundamental in the Chilean State: its class character.

Thus the armed forces played a passive role from November 1970 to October 1972, and after that their participation was indispensable to assure continuity of the institutional system in the face of the confrontation between powers, programs, and classes in Chilean society. With the whole process moving down a blind alley where one of the two forces had to be defeated for the other to survive, the military crushed the popular movement to assure the continuance of capitalism.

The institutions proved to be a kind that concealed the essence of the fruit—the capitalist social and economic system, which can assume many political forms without losing its content.

1. *El Mercurio* (Santiago de Chile), October 26, 1972.
2. Statement by Interior Minister Gerardo Espinoza, *El Mercurio*, March 31, 1973.
3. Quoted in *Arauco* magazine (Buenos Aires), July 1974.
4. *El Mercurio*, May 11, 1973.
5. *El Mercurio*, June 1, 1973.
6. *El Mercurio*, May 18, 1973.
7. *El Mercurio*, May 18, 1973.
8. *El Mercurio*, June 14, 1973.
9. Statement by Carlos Briones, *El Mercurio*, July 10, 1973.
10. Statement by the Democratic Confederation, *El Mercurio*, July 7, 1973.
11. *El Mercurio*, August 23, 1973.
12. Study by U.S. sociologist Roy Allen Hansen, "Military Culture and Organizational Decline," cited by Pío García in *Las Fuerzas Armadas y el Golpe de Estado en Chile* (Mexico: Siglo XXI, 1974).
13. *Newsweek*, September 24, 1973.
14. *Chile Hoy* (Santiago de Chile), No. 23, November 17, 1972.
15. *El Mercurio*, March 21, 1973.
16. Statements by Luis Corvalán, *El Mercurio*, March 23, 1973.
17. *El Mercurio*, December 28, 1972.
18. *El Mercurio*, December 28, 1972.
19. *El Mercurio*, March 14, 1973.
20. Statement by Carlos Prats, *El Mercurio*, April 27, 1973.
21. *El Mercurio*, May 29, 1973.
22. *Chile Hoy*, July 15, 1973.

9 SEPTEMBER 1973: THE TRIUMPH OF REACTION

The election results in March 1973 banished all doubt that the direction of a society depends on the relationship of forces between classes, and that votes serve to record numerically the classes' respective weights at a given moment but not to decide the course of events.

Of this the forces of reaction were fully aware, especially the direct representatives of the employer associations who, immediately after the bourgeoisie's "parliamentary" scheme failed, put new intensity into their appeals to the armed forces and their challenge of the government's legality.

The government, taking a strictly defensive stance, sought to check the class struggle with a view to implementing the often frustrated plan of an agreement with the "middle classes" via transactions with Christian Democracy. For this President Allende on March 28 named a Socialist in whom he had complete confidence as interior minister in a new cabinet, whose express task was to bring the conflicting interests together through legal channels: "The opposition and the government parties must understand that the president of the republic will use every means to avoid violence, and all those in any sector who seek to unleash it will find in the decision of the executive a barrier to prevent a confrontation in this country."[1]

In those same days a Communist Party Central Committee Plenum described the MIR as "a divisive factor within the popular movement, which should be combated to keep it from winning any sector of the people for its suicidal policy." In the Socialist Party Plenum, those favoring a conciliatory line with the bourgeoisie and Christian Democracy were considerably strengthened.

The government's difficulties with the two poles of society made the task it set itself extremely hard to implement. The popular movement was in rebellion against a situation that offered none of the advantages of socialism and most of the evils of capitalism, with inflation and hoarding that presented a daily threat to the masses' purchasing power. On April 4 pitched battles broke out in the streets of the Vicuña Mackenna district, due to the *carabineros'* harsh repression of demonstrating *pobladores.*

Meanwhile the bourgeoisie and Christian Democracy were putting up much tougher resistance to government policy. On April 10 the government sent to the comptroller's office a Decree of Insistence to implement requisitioning of some important industries programmed from the outset for the social sector. SOFOFA called this "one step more in the Marxist escalation that has followed the departure of the military ministers [from the cabinet] ," and added: "The measure is typically totalitarian, imposed as it is by an abuse of power disregarding the opinion of Congress, of the comptroller's office, or of the national majorities."[2]

SOFOFA was in almost perfect harmony with Christian Democratic party president Renán Fuentealba, who said on the same day: "The government is taking a series of measures which amount to genuine aggression, a war it has declared against democracy. These measures are the attacks against the national Congress . . . and pulling such legal strings as the Decrees of Insistence to grab industries for the social sector."[3]

For its part, the National Party, speaking for the most resolute element of the bourgeois opposition, said: ". . . The moment has come for Congress . . . to declare that the government has finally lost its authority and legitimacy. . . . No one is obliged to respect nor continue obeying an authority that neither respects nor obeys the country's laws."[4]

Red lights were flashing everywhere, which the government and "Chilean road to socialism" partisans in Popular Unity unrealistically refused to see. Unable to change their policy, powerless to buttress themselves on the revolutionary energy of the masses, they saw no other course than a headlong one toward the already yawning abyss. All the meager advantages that the "institutional road" had afforded were now seen to be insignificant in the face of the reactionary escalation and the impossibility of fighting it with the weapons of bourgeois-democratic legality. Each day what had been a fortress was more and more plainly becoming the source of the government's—and even more so the popular movement's—weakness. Until September 11 this situation would increasingly resemble the agonies of a sick man being destroyed by the "remedies" administered to him.

In April the El Teniente copper-mine workers called a strike that laid bare some key errors in Popular Unity's ideological model, for here was a numerous and concentrated sector of the proletariat, the best example of what could be called Chile's labor aristocracy, succumbing to the slogans, leadership, and plans of the bourgeoisie. The strike, lasting seventy-seven days, was the first sign of the corrosion of certain popular strata who, making their own hay out of the government's loss of authority, came out with strictly economistic demands.

The opposition kept up the offensive against government positions on many fronts simultaneously: the plan to modernize and democratize education, the JAPs, the intervened enterprises now in the social sector, the violence for which the opposition was responsible and the Left was lamed, the illegal, unlicensed subsidiary of Catholic University's TV channel. These were the main storm centers precisely because the bourgeoisie used the state mechanisms which it controlled, and the mass media which it owned, to maintain the initiative and force the government into a nonstop campaign of denials and explanations which made it highly vulnerable. Behind this weakness was the lack of an alternative model for the popular movement. Obliged to respect bourgeois legality, the executive power and its administration had to squeeze out the last drop of the poison they had too hastily labeled as a remedy, while the Right freely used and abused an institutional context that it openly benefited from.

At the end of April Santiago's streets became battlegrounds, with hundreds wounded and arrested in clashes provoked by the vandalism of Christian Democratic and National Party students commingled with Patria y Libertad's hired thugs. On April 28 CUT called on the workers to demonstrate in response to the right-wing provocations, and a young Communist worker was murdered, thrown from the windows of Christian Democracy's central headquarters.

In this atmosphere of extreme tension May Day was celebrated without the presence of Cardinal Silva Henríquez, who announced his "deep pain" at not attending as he had done the previous year. "As bishop and priest," he explained, "I must be the center of unity for my people." This sadly did not keep the priest Raúl Hasbún from conducting an incredible antipeople and antigovernment campaign on the Catholic University TV channel, in which he lined up with the most extreme and rabid fascists. At the May Day demonstration President Allende did not fail to take a stand against the threat of civil war openly made by the employer guilds: "We are not afraid of it, we know that the forces of the people and the loyalty of the armed forces of order permit us to look ahead with tranquillity."[5] But these verbal tranquilizers confused only the workers, not their enemies, for polarization of the country was advancing like an express train and anyone trying to brake or intercept it was violently hurled aside.

From May 14 the "hard-core" Christian Democrats behind Frei took their party's helm, with Senator Patricio Aylwin as party president. Aylwin, who had been accustomed to using such expressions as "economic disaster," "totalitarian tendencies of the government," "new state bureaucracy," "fight Popular Unity's attempt to install the dictatorship of the stomach," now dotted the i's thus: "In face of the resurgence of violence in our country, the Christian Democratic National Committee reiterates the necessity of strict compliance with the Arms Control Law, and suggests to the armed forces the appropriateness of using every means provided for that legal body to prevent the existence or proliferation of armed groups. . . ."[6]

The popular parties tried to defend their gains but were not in a position to put forward an alternative; bourgeois legality and institutionality tied their hands while tension continued to mount sharply. In mid-June the copper miners were still on strike and in the streets of Santiago and other cities there were new and more violent confrontations. Physicians declared a strike; the Chamber of Deputies accused the ministers of economy, labor, and mining of unconstitutional behavior, deposed them, and embarked on the necessary procedures to do likewise with the interior minister; and a Supreme Court judge pronounced the government's general secretary a criminal. Simultaneously the bishops of Santiago, Valparaíso, Linares, Rancagua, San Felipe, and Talca issued this joint declaration: "There are changes that go in a mistaken direction when they are inspired by materialist conceptions. . . . Chile is like a country scourged by war."[7]

As a sample of the extreme weakness with which capitalist institutions had infected the government, the following instructions were sent by the government's general secretary to the ministers of state, under-secretaries, and commissioners:

> As from today audiences will not be granted to parliamentarians, leaders, or other personnel of the National Party. . . . The said political organization has placed itself outside the constitutional and legal provisions regulating the democratic harmony of the country by declaring that the president of the Republic has infringed the law in the exercise of his functions and by stating that citizens have no obligation to respect or obey the government. . . . Such a statement is tantamount to sedition. [8]

Shall we say that, in the face of sedition, the "punishment" of denying audiences to the bourgeois party which in those very days was fostering and organizing plans for the coup d'état seems a little out of proportion? But there was little more the government could do within legality, since courts and Congress paid little attention to the illegalities of right-wing organizations.

CUT staged a giant progovernment demonstration on June 21, at which ringing calls of "get tough with the enemy," "power for the workers," and "create, create popular power" showed a distinct change in the mind of the masses: they were really beginning to question the limitations of institutionality while at the same time defending the government, for they well knew it had been the dam against the revanchist floodwaters of the bourgeoisie. The contradiction was like a snarled knot, for as we have shown, the dam was strictly defensive. Its foundations were being progressively undermined as the opposition line developed clearer contours—by now more and more openly putschist, as a very few more days would show.

In effect, on June 29 the streets of downtown Santiago reverberated with the clatter of lumbering tanks, the thunder of guns, and stutter of machine guns. The 2nd Armored Regiment had mutinied in collusion with the fascist movement Patria y Libertad. It bombarded the Moneda (Presidential) Palace and attacked the defense ministry building in an adventure which, for reasons never wholly explained, other committed regiments failed to support. Actually, while it was going on, putschist officers, particularly of the navy and air force, were openly debating whether they should join in and set up a military dictatorship. All the evidence suggests that the army putschists had not yet fully matured their plans and that this finally decided them to stay out of the June 29 affair, which was crushed by some regiments under General Prats's personal command. Prats maintained his constitutional convictions to the end.

A journalist on the scene described this revealing incident:

> On the Alameda in the direction of Arturo Prat [Street], the leftist groups got thicker and thicker. On the street in front of the Club de la Unión they all milled around a tall figure, José Tohá, who was surrounded by three soldiers and headed a large military column:
>
> "*Viva* the minister of defense! *Viva* Tohá!"
>
> Everyone wanted to shake his hand or embrace him, but the three soldiers protected him. A young man approached excitedly and, holding out his hands to one of the soldiers, cried:
>
> "Be a good fellow and let me have that little popgun! . . ."
>
> "Here's how I'll let you have it," replied the soldier aggressively, pointing his rifle at the youth.
>
> Tohá sternly reprimanded the young man for letting his enthusiasm run away with him . . .
>
> On the sidewalk another large group shouted *Vivas!* for the soldiers and for Tohá the minister. General Prats came up:
>
> "Go away, please, go away. There are still many problems to solve. Let us work in peace."[9]

Thus the popular government's defense minister, a Socialist, and the commander-in-chief, unchallenged head of the military "constitutionalists," concurred fully and expressed clearly the limitations and weaknesses of their position. When the coup finally came, that soldier would not be at Tohá's side to defend him, and the civilian, the young leftist who wanted a gun, would certainly not have one. Tohá and Prats were convinced that the confrontations were exclusively an internal affair of the armed forces, that the workers had nothing to do with them and should "let them work in peace." On September 11, when the relation of forces within the armed institutions was to turn decisively in the putschists' favor, it would be primarily due to the executive's policy of isolating the military from the rest of society and from the class struggle. It was precisely this isolation which fueled the disciplinary and hierarchical machinery of an organism structured by the capitalist state. This was what made impossible any solidarity between workers in struggle against the bourgeoisie and soldiers, NCOs, and sectors of officers who had class and material interests in common with the masses. To make matters worse, when the hour struck for the definitive breakdown of institutionality, the workers and left militants would not be able to fight since they would face the repressive machine with empty hands. And the responsibility lay with a policy that blindly idealized military "professionalism" even after the putschists' presence in all of the country's barracks had become common knowledge.

Far from being turned into an opportunity to strike at the military "institutionalists" or to disarm or at least weaken them, the abortive June 29 *tancazo* marked the beginning of accelerated conspiratorial palavers among all reactionary groups, political, economic, and military.

Patria y Libertad, the fascistic movement which admitted its complicity with the apprentice putschists, declared that "various other military units that had previously shown us support" were also involved. However, the Congress led by Frei, purportedly the institutional bastion against the executive's "undermining" actions, denied to the executive the invocation of the State of Siege Law which "would have placed at its disposal elements to ensure a thorough investigation of the attempted subversion." And on July 3, thanks to a majority formed in it by National Party and Christian Democratic members, the Chamber of Deputies dismissed the interior minister—just five days after the frustrated military coup! Reaction no longer concealed its contempt for prevailing institutions and stepped up its attack against a glaringly vulnerable government which remained almost totally passive.

But if the government was bogged down in legality, the workers were not; their response to the *tancazo* was the occupation of many enterprises and a renewed impetus to the development of popular power organizations. Moving well ahead of the Left parties' directives, workers in factories, *pobladores* in their communities, miners, campesinos in central and south Chile, teachers, health workers, and students threw themselves with fresh energy into strengthening their new structures, developing *comandos comunales,* reactivating campesino councils, securing *cordones industriales* and beginning to coordinate them. At the rank-and-file level the most conscious and advanced sectors realized that confrontation was now inevitable, that an attempt to capture total power was the only alternative to losing all that had so far been won.

This was not an analysis made by the government and the top

echelons of Popular Unity. Immediately following the thwarted coup a new cabinet was formed, headed by an official who had held major posts in the administrations of Eduardo Frei and the conservative Jorge Alessandri. Its basic mission was to facilitate a "dialogue" with Christian Democracy and provide maximum guarantees for it. This was the only strategy of a government in which the Communist Party predominated:

> But there is room for dialogue with the majority of citizens. There are people who are not with the government but still don't want it overthrown, who are convinced that Chile must not return to the past, that changes are needed and civil war must be avoided. Certainly there is room for dialogue with people who think in that way, and finally perhaps some sort of understanding. . . .[10]

These appeals to the chief opposition party were destined to fall into a void. On the same day, the three branches of the armed forces launched a wave of violent raids in Santiago and other cities such as Punta Arenas and Osorno, which took on the character of territory occupied by an enemy of the population. And meanwhile, with a helping Christian Democratic hand, the employers began working out a new strike like that of October, in which truckers, physicians, and some maritime unions would participate.

In the Socialist Party there were various shades of opinion. While Altamirano "categorically" rejected "any dialogue with reactionary, counter-revolutionary parties and leaderships" (referring to the government's efforts for new talks with Christian Democracy), Socialist undersecretary Sepúlveda said:

> We are part of the government and hence cannot, at a given stage of its movement, simply deprive it of the machinery it needs to move. We are also a supportive base of the government. There is a difference of criterion as to the perspective but nothing opportunistic in the fact that we say the perspective should be developed. We do not consider that in a multiparty government such as ours—where the criterion of one group cannot predominate, nor can a single party, so to speak, put the others and the government in a bind—that it is opportunistic to say, no, we do not believe it is opportunism to let the majority decide what is to be done.[11]

In other words the Socialist leadership was protesting, but once again—and in the most dramatic hours of the Chilean process—would end up submitting to the Communists' policies and tactics. What was at stake was no less than the fate of the revolution and of the Chilean workers, yet in that situation the Socialist leadership felt that the majority should dispose of all the tools to continue its hopeless attempts at conciliation.

MIR's position at this time coincided with that of MAPU, the Christian Left, and the great majority of Socialist Party sections and regional groups:

> A step back is not necessary in order to take two steps forward. The working class and the people need no truce or breathing spell today. The boss classes do need a truce to develop their tactical timetable. Today nothing would be more dangerous and suicidal than to abandon positions that have been won and to declare a truce. Like it or not, say it or not, that would mean demoralizing, disorganizing, and dividing the working class and the people, obliging them to retreat, and hence implacably bringing down on them the full bloody force of the boss classes. . . .[12]

As things turned out, while among the officers the balance turned clearly in the putschists' favor, and the elements under Christian Democratic influence converged with those influenced by the National Party and Patria y Libertad, something new occurred early in July: NCOs and rank-and-file soldiers, who in certain areas resisted joining in the reactionary plottings, began to get together.

What they were discussing was how to open up all the hatches that prevented the revolutionary forces from throwing legality overboard, since representatives of the bourgeoisie were openly destroying that legality. The situation throughout July did not ensure success for this move but did make it a possibility under far better conditions than obtained in the final showdown in September. But in that situation the government and Popular Unity leadership, even on the brink of the abyss to which their policies had brought them, remained firm in their respect for bourgeois institutionality and for the armed forces' "professionalism."

To which we must add that in the decisive hours, as it confronted the strategy developed by the rightists, who were all set to smash the popular movement, the movement was in a state of complete disorientation and demoralization.

The fundamental weapon was lacking: a political organization that could unify the workers' struggles, give them a global and national perspective, and lead theoretically and practically to implementation of all necessary material measures. At that juncture the Left revolutionary sectors revealed all of their organic and political inability to generate a vanguard leadership for the labor movement.

The left wing of the Socialist Party ultimately showed itself to be an "attitude," a tendency spread all through the party, incapable of promoting actions and lines independent of the official leadership, much less of compelling it to line up with the majority positions of the membership. Its practice consisted of the scattered efforts of members to develop the various expressions of popular power, but these activities reflected no overall plan nor any center to coordinate and concentrate them. The left wing of the Socialist Party was primarily centered around most of the Socialist Party regional committees, but they directed activities only within their own geographical areas, since there was no coordination between the various committees whose theoretical strategic positions differed basically from the majority policies of the national party leadership.

MIR and MAPU for their part did not develop substantially as parties, had no appreciable mass influence, were not rooted in the labor movement, and their ranks produced few leaders. Nor did they put forward a coherent and integrating line that could have brought workers together behind it.

Thus the revolutionary Left was scattered among various organizations, none of which could, by itself, present an alternative program to those of reaction and of reformism. The root cause of this was the subordination within the mass movement of the revolutionary Left line to that of the Communists allied with petty-bourgeois reformists. All through the process we have observed different sectors, especially of the Socialist Party, setting out to promote, radicalize, and speed up a program that other forces were implementing, but never presenting to the masses, for discussion by the workers, a tactically and strategically worked-out plan embracing all of the society's problems. Lacking such a plan, these sectors were limited to criticizing and rejecting policies of the government and Popular Unity leaders, but they had no common denominator that could unify them in a challenge to the popular movement's leadership. All of this is inextricably locked into the

Socialist Party's history, with its ambiguities, its mixture of different tendencies on all levels—in short, the absence from it of any single current that could have responsibly opposed the government line and woven the scattered tactical threads into a solid alternative to a Central Committee that always ended up compromising with the Communists.

For these reasons the revolutionary Left never went beyond being a tendency, a reflection of broad sectors of the popular movement, a part of the working masses existing chiefly inside Popular Unity but also outside it, but never maturing into a single concept, an alternative all-embracing program, nor managing to coordinate its forces—much less to take over effectively the leadership of the mass movement and give it a drastically different orientation. It lucidly argued against, challenged, and criticized the "politico-institutional road" concept, but did not put forward a body of tactical and strategic propositions which would add up to an overall plan for transforming society. It was unable to create a Leninist axis challenging the management of the process. In the last analysis the Left revolutionary tendencies' participation in the process led by the government and Popular Unity leadership presaged their own destruction. This was in no way inevitable, for after October 1972 the maturing of the working-class vanguard offered conditions for its development and organic growth. But the slogans "Defend the Government" and "Unity of the Workers," which had certainly been correct and proper in a given context, came to represent defense and unity around a line that was definitely responsible for the tragic outcome.

Building a revolutionary party was the Chilean working class's unfinished task and the weakest link in the chain the workers forged to transform society. In consequence the program essentially directed by the Communist Party went forward with considerable autonomy, limited only on the Left by the dynamic radicalization of the mass movement. Thus when the decisive period began after June 29, the *cordones* expressed and attracted what was most advanced in the urban proletariat, and they tried to create a power alternative with almost empty hands. But the nonexistence of a party that could generalize its experiences and give the most conscious workers the comprehensive, unifying thrust for such a policy made the necessary take-off impossible for popular power.

And on the ideological level there was a definite acceptance in practice of all the nondialectical, non-Leninist models advocated and implemented by the government and the Communist Party for Chilean society's transition to socialism. Thus, with respect to using bourgeois-democratic institutionality, the broad masses accepted a concept implying their own subjection to it—their own confinement within its boundaries. Revolutionary Left currents were incapable of hoisting and keeping aloft a different banner, one that would imply convincing and organizing the workers' vanguard around the need to destroy the capitalist state. Theories were indeed articulated, but they did not take on coherent form in an overall alternative formulation, let alone a different tactic. In fact we can say that, to some extent and for a certain time, Left sectors of the Socialist Party seemed confused and convinced by the possibilities of great advances within this legality; that while they knew confrontation was inevitable, they thought it belonged to a stage that was still remote. After the *tancazo* there was a feverish search for solutions, perspectives, tactics, organization, and methods. But a people without traditions of armed struggle, imbued for decades with respect for state institutions not only by the bourgeoisie but by the Left, daunted by a reality that was suddenly hammering them, and without any solidly organized political leadership to offer them an insurrectionary way out, was already defeated and abandoned before September 11.

Throughout July the military paraded their power in exhibitions of brutality, mainly to intimidate the vanguard workers in the *cordones,* while "constitutionalist" army officers were ousted and resistance in the navy was destroyed by the arrest and torture of loyal petty officers. Simultaneously and with machinelike precision, reaction was using all institutional means to legitimize the approaching coup, and the petty-bourgeois "guilds" went all-out to provoke chaos and set the stage for armed intervention. Patria y Libertad was inspiring a wave of violence and sabotage and at the end of the month came the strikes of the truckers, physicians, and other professional groups.

Meanwhile, on July 30, the government with sublime obstinacy began a new "dialogue" with the Christian Democrats, who set draconian conditions. *El Mercurio* reported on that day what those "non-negotiable" conditions were:

(1) Complete restoration of institutionality, constitutional norms and democratic coexistence to be fully operative. (2) Promulgation of those constitutional reforms still pending due to executive

objections, with the opposition parties' absolute majority as a quorum. (3) Reform of industries taken over by order of CUT. (4) Intensification of the campaign to disarm political, union, or civil groups. (5) Implementation of these four points to be guaranteed by installing a cabinet with institutional representation of the armed forces.[13]

In a nutshell, Christian Democracy proposed the submission of the executive power to a Congress in which bourgeois interests had majority representation, settling once and for all in the bourgeoisie's favor the conflict on big industrial holdings, and also aimed at crushing the popular movement—all of this with the military's active presence controlling the president from inside the cabinet. In a communication to Allende a few hours later, Christian Democratic chief Aylwin made even more explicit his aim of bringing the fragile government to its knees:

> Your Excellency would secure his constitutional authority and preserve the Republic's institutional stability if he set up a ministry with institutional participation by the armed forces, with sufficient powers in high and middle offices to assure effective implementation of Your Excellency's decisions within the Constitution and laws, applied equally to all.[14]

That is, Christian Democracy proposed to apply to Chile a formula similar to the one then being applied to Uruguay, by which the constitutional president had become the puppet of military reactionaries. The proposal, described as a "white coup d'état," was not accepted, but a new cabinet was formed on August 9 which, again including the commanders-in-chief of the three armed forces plus the director general of *carabineros,* left the door ajar for the continuance of the talks. What possibilities of understanding this offered were promptly blocked by Senate president Frei who said: "This government has led the country to catastrophe and now, with a clever and audacious move, uses the armed forces to saddle them with this disaster and oblige them to face the consequences of a fatal policy for which they are in no way responsible."[15]

By then all the preparatory mechanisms for the coup were revving up with well-greased gears. National Party youth gangs were ravaging the center of the capital with the active participation of high school students led by Christian Democracy; each day brought more terrorist and sabotage actions; the truckers' strike completely dislocated the country; storekeepers, nearly all physicians, and other professionals were on indefinite strike; and the military intensified its efforts to intimidate the workers throughout the country.

In this final phase the popular movement was desperately trying to conserve its strength and generate new centers of alternative power to confront the military offensive. But the Left parties' vacillations and the government's conciliatory course continued to leave their mark. The will and energy of the masses cannot be lightly trifled with; the relationships of forces in decisive situations are extremely fluid and changeable. The working class was not isolated but retained its allies in broad sectors of *pobladores*, campesinos, and white-collar public and private employees. But to a great extent the determination and initiative shown by the workers right after the *tancazo* had been uselessly corroded and diluted, due to all the maneuverings that not only did not promote their activity but rather sought a way out through superstructural agreements with the enemy—ministerial changes purportedly offering "democratic guarantees" to people without the remotest democratic intentions, conciliation of social interests that were irreconcilable, and efforts to reach a "political solution" precisely with those who demanded military preponderance in running the country.

As August neared its end Christian Democrats and Nationalists had painstakingly achieved all the objectives of their convergent tactic: to challenge the government's legitimacy and legality head-on, generate a mass movement to back up their seditious line, sap the strength and firmness of the workers who stood behind the popular government, and deepen and broaden pro-putschist sentiment in the three branches of the armed institutions.

And on August 23 Carlos Prats resigned both as commander-in-chief and as defense minister:

> . . . Having become aware in these past days that my detractors have succeeded in beclouding the judgment of a sector of army officers, I have felt it the duty of a soldier with firm principles not to make myself a factor in the breakdown of institutional discipline and dislocation of the state of law, nor to serve as a pretext for those who seek the overthrow of the constitutional government.[16]

Prats's resignation in fact served none of these objectives. There were enough "pretexts" already for the impending action of the putschists. Prats's successor was General Pinochet. Thus a cycle was completed within military institutionality, for the "constitutionalist" generals had hampered the discussion among NCOs and rank and file and disheartened the officers loyal to the government, while at the same time failing to maintain discipline among the "institutionalists," who by now were almost brazenly preparing to seize power.

With the exit of Prats the government's military defeat was sealed even before the coup, which would meet with little resistance in the armed forces and would open the doors to an orgy of reactionary and totalitarian vengeance upon workers and leftists.

Events sped toward the climax. The government's death agonies were approaching their end. The general chaos provoked by the political opposition and the bourgeois "guilds" held the country in semi-paralysis; workers, *pobladores*, campesinos, and other popular strata were left defenseless by the military offensive—under the pretext of the Arms Control Law—which continued until the constitutional government's last days.

On September 4 the Christian Democrats' National Council agreed to present constitutional charges against the whole body of ministers of state, to get rid of the lot all at once. On the same day Santiago saw an immense demonstration commemorating the third anniversary of the popular victory—more than a million Chileans to whom Salvador Allende spoke these strange and pathetic words:

> Workers of Chile: winter is coming to an end and promising economic horizons are opening up for us. In the last years we have been punished by the low price of copper on the world market. Now it is bringing high prices which will provide us with the hard currency necessary for the importation of raw materials and consumer goods. In August production at the Chiquicamata mine was the highest in its history. The area sown this winter is double that of last year. We must repeat this with the spring sowings. Thus greater mining, agricultural, and industrial production and the workers' organization and creative capacity will hold back inflation and shortages in the coming year. . . .

Reality had shown that this approach embodied a mistaken concept of the connection between economic, social, and political processes.

Already in reality the "Battle of Production" inspired by the Communist Party had failed to reach its goals. The workers had made greater efforts than ever and production had risen in many areas: at the end of 1972, as we recall, it was 15 percent higher in the social sector than in 1971. But such means could never halt shortages and inflation, for these reflected on the one hand a drive for the highest profit-rate in the specific conditions of Chile's economic process, and on the other a deliberate policy of the owners of capital.

When Allende spoke these words, they were already devoid of all meaning. The Commitment and will of the multitude were totally insufficient to halt the determined march of reaction and the power of the armed forces.

At 8 AM on September 11 radio stations began broadcasting this message:

> In view of (1) the extremely grave social and moral crisis through which the country is passing, (2) the government's inability to control chaos, (3) the continuous growth of paramilitary groups trained by the Popular Unity parties, which will inevitably lead the people of Chile into civil war, the armed forces and *carabineros* have decided: 1. the president of the Republic must immediately surrender his office to the armed forces and *carabineros* of Chile; 2. the armed forces and *carabineros* stand united to begin the historic and responsible mission of fighting for the liberty of the motherland and preventing our country from falling under the Marxist yoke, and seeking to restore order and institutionality; 3. the workers of Chile may rest assured that the economic and social gains they have achieved until now will suffer no basic modifications; 4. the pro–Popular Unity press, radio, and TV must suspend their informational activities from this instant, otherwise they will receive punishment by air and by land; 5. the people of Santiago must remain in their homes to avoid becoming innocent victims.[17]

On that same day, personally fighting the army and air forces which attacked the Moneda Palace, Salvador Allende, constitutional president of Chile, fell, murdered by the institutionality which he had respected to the end, achieving in that dramatic hour the dialectical negation and transcendence of the process he had embodied.

In the face of these events I can only say to the workers: I will not resign. Standing where I do on this historic journey, I will pay with my life for the loyalty of the people, and I say to them that I know that the seed we will hand on to the good conscience of thousands and thousands of Chileans cannot and will not be destroyed. They have the force, they can subdue us, but social processes are not halted by crime or by force. History is ours and it is the people who make it.[18]

Thus tragically began the most difficult hours in all history for the people of Chile who, because of the line applied by the majority leadership of Popular Unity, had ended up materially, politically, and ideologically disarmed.

1. *El Mercurio* (Santiago de Chile), March 29, 1973.
2. *El Mercurio*, April 11, 1973.
3. Ibid.
4. *El Mercurio*, April 15, 1973.
5. *El Mercurio*, May 2, 1973.
6. *El Mercurio*, May 14, 1973.
7. *El Mercurio*, June 21, 1973.
8. Ibid.
9. José Cayuela, in *Chile Hoy* (Santiago de Chile), July 6, 1973.
10. Luis Corvalán at the Teatro Caupolicán, July 7, 1973.
11. Adonis Sepúlveda in *Chile Hoy*, August 10, 1973.
12. Miguel Enríquez, in *Chile Hoy* July 6, 1973.
13. *El Mercurio*, July 31, 1973.
14. *El Mercurio*, August 3, 1973.
15. *El Mercurio*, August 18, 1973.
16. *Chile Hoy*, August 31, 1973.
17. *El Mercurio*, September 12, 1973.
18. Quoted in *Arauco* magazine (Buenos Aires), No. 1, July 1974.

10 A CHILEAN ROAD TO SOCIALISM?

The Popular Unity program was the result of compromise between different tendencies. Chief of these were the Communist Party line expressed in the National Liberation Front thesis, the petty-bourgeois reformist tendency which carried particular weight in sectors of the government, and a workers' revolutionary position taken by part of the Socialist Party, MAPU, and the Christian Left, and allied at certain times with the MIR.

Despite its ambiguity on some points and especially on the problem of power, the latter program correctly evaluated Chilean society and the steps necessary to develop a revolutionary policy, with the presidency of the Republic at the service of the popular struggle and of a socialist strategy. But from the first months the reformist tendencies allied themselves with and followed the Communist Party's gradualist line, gaining net ascendancy in the Popular Unity and government leadership for a policy that was not revolutionary and was in contradiction with basic points of the common program. Thus the tactic that was followed, especially after the Lo Curro meeting in June 1972, was the responsibility of one sector of Popular Unity: it undertook a historic task which, in circumstances offering all the prerequisites previously outlined as necessary, ended in failure.

The so-called Chilean "road to socialism" or "politico-institutional road," originating in the strategy devised by the Communist Party at its Tenth Congress in 1956, was implemented and developed under the leadership of the Communist-reformist alliance within Popular Unity during the whole period from November 1970 to September 1973. The revolutionary groupings had no responsibility for the three chief aspects that sealed the government's doom: (1) the class-alliance plan, (2) the policy toward the armed forces, (3) the use of the institutional apparatus.

The class-alliance plan was spelled out in the Popular Unity government's basic program, especially in the "new economy" or "transition economy" concept which contemplated, side by side with a "dominant social sector," a mixed sector combining state and private capital and a private-property sector including most of Chile's 30,500 industrial firms, nearly all commercial enterprises, and all agricultural holdings of less than the equivalent of eighty irrigated hectares. For these enterprises "the state will procure the necessary finance and technical aid, so that they may fulfill their important function in the national economy. . . ." Thus the program defended and guaranteed the permanence and development of small and middle proprietors' interests. In addition to these economic formulations, the program proposed to establish a class alliance of proletariat and other nonpropertied working strata with the small and middle bourgeoisie, through organic participation of the Radical and Social Democratic parties and of Independent Popular Action which represented them in Popular Unity and the government. The repeated vows to respect the civic system constituted a full political guarantee for the expression and permanence of an important sector of the Chilean bourgeoisie.

The worker-bourgeois class alliance was not altogether new: ever since 1938 parties representing the organized majority in the exploited classes had participated in various successive governments. But there was a distinct difference between the Popular Front of 1938 and the Popular Unity of 1970: the latter came into being under the hegemony of workers' parties and of a Socialist president, and with the explicit perspective of starting to build socialism. That is, while the previous alliance had developed under the leadership of a fraction of the bourgeoisie, this one proposed to attain its objectives through a coalition basically led by the Communist Party and its petty-bourgeois reformist allies but also containing a significant revolutionary grouping.

The class-alliance plan had two aspects, economic and political. On the economic level it seemed viable through 1971 and part of 1972, when the workers' rising buying power boosted the profits of small and middle merchants, farmers, and industrialists. But events took an unexpected and disillusioning turn: suddenly inflation, hoarding, and speculation struck Chile. Clearly part of the explanation was that with the laws of the capitalist system remaining in full force, the rise of demand above supply had to produce those results. The reaction of all propertied groups—big, middle, and small—under the baton of finance capital, and duly stimulated by the bourgeois mass media, was to try for the highest rate of profit, and this they found in the hoarding of all consumer goods and consequent speculation. Chile became a huge corrupt market in which anyone with an ounce of capital trafficked in what the workers needed and hoped to buy. The necessary production-raising investments ingenuously expected by Popular Unity's technicians did not materialize. The private sector's profits were deflected into the black market, and the Chilean state—badly hit by low copper prices, the imperialist financial blockade, and constantly rising internal demand for imported consumer goods—could not itself find the necessary investment capital.

Fully maintained while capitalist supply and demand continued, the Chilean economy went into an accelerated and uncontrolled plunge which, within the system, only a brutal limitation of the workers' buying power could halt.

Another important factor helped prevent the proposed alliance: the middle bourgeoisie's deep distrust of the government's capacity and/or desire to hold the popular movement within "legal" bounds and the limits envisaged by its leaders. Actually the government tried over and over again to forge the alliance with the "middle classes," showing steadfast readiness to legislate and to reach agreements with Christian Democracy. It spurned the opportunity offered by the April 1971 elections to speed the processes contemplated in its program, precisely in order "not to frighten the middle classes," and the Communist Party rejected the idea of a plebiscite.

In April and particularly in June of 1972, coinciding with cabinet changes and promises to "consolidate" the situation—that is, to slow down formation of the social sector—there were talks with Christian Democracy which almost reached agreement but were aborted at the last minute by Frei, "boss" of that party. Then, following the popular victory over the employer guilds in October, the government again showed its benevolence by forming a ministry with military men in top posts and sending to Congress the "Millas Plan" broadly guaranteeing bourgeois property. Through 1973 the government continued the talks, seeking but never achieving agreement with Christian Democracy as the representative of the "middle classes." After the June 1973 *tancazo* the government even tried to put Christian Democrat Fernando Castillo Velasco in the cabinet but his party would not hear of it. Finally in August, when tension reached its height, the government and Popular Unity made another try for "dialogue" to reach an understanding with a fraction of the bourgeoisie, and again it fell to Frei to head this off.

In sum, the Communist Party's alliance with petty-bourgeois reformism had a completely free hand in the government and also in Popular Unity to pursue a policy of economic and political understanding with the "middle classes," and its failure must be attributed to the strategy as a whole.

The policy toward the armed forces was just as fully the responsibility of the dominant sector in the government and Popular Unity, who to the very end upheld the thesis of military "professionalism" and respect for the Constitution. The decisions to bring the military into the cabinet and administration were part of the tactic of strengthening the "patriotic" and "constitutionalist" sectors. The failure of this became evident late in the day but in dramatic terms, with savage and generalized repression. The attempt to recover stability through the military after the bourgeois semi-insurrection in October 1972 did nothing to implement the class-alliance plan, but on the contrary weakened the military "constitutionalists" who failed to achieve "social peace." As the role of the military grew in importance, the government could only reaffirm the traditional myths of the dominant ideology, and after the June 1973 *tancazo* the Communist Party daily *El Siglo* had a whole page defending the glories of the army. Simultaneously appeared the slogan "No to Civil War," which was finally consummated by completing the demobilization of the workers and leaving the resolution of the struggle—the fate of Chile's revolutionary process—to the relation of forces within the armed institutions. As a corollary to this line, when naval petty officers and enlisted men put up resistance, it was precisely the government that undertook to discourage their struggle against the putschists. Sectors of Popular Unity, specifically of the Socialist Party and MAPU, as well as the MIR, issued calls for disobedience which came too late and failed in their objective. By then the reactionaries had already had all the time necessary to unify almost all of the armed apparatuses behind the plot that would surface on September 11.

The government's and the Communists' policy of keeping a fraction of the armed forces in "constitutionalist" positions would prove a total failure, while at the same time the vacillations and submissions to this line stopped the possibility of a deeper split when the revolutionary Left directed its appeal to the military. Thus was again confirmed the historic experience of the impossibility of fighting against modern armed forces and the indispensability of splitting them if revolutionary bids for power are to succeed. By never attempting such a policy the government led events straight as an arrow to the fascistic violence that followed the June 29 putsch and the raids under pretext of the Arms Control Law. True, the armed forces were divided for a long time, but the division was between "constitutionalists" and "institutionalists," that is, between reformists and putschists. And the government line led directly to reinforcement of the reactionary positions until the "constitutionalists" became weak enough to be easily swept aside. That is the story of the government's military policy.

Resort to the institutions of the Chilean bourgeois-democratic state soon showed its limitations as a device for implementing Popular Unity's program. It did open the door into the state system for the workers' parties, "legitimizing" their demands in institutional terms and putting important tools into the hands of the popular movement. But it is also true that it barricaded the movement within the iron ring of a body of laws and mechanisms planned and elaborated precisely for the subjection of the dominated classes to bourgeois hegemony. Reaction had no qualms about violating and ignoring the Constitution on various occasions, through the actions of Congress (reform of the Fundamental Law by simple majority, ignoring the Constitutional Tribunal), of the judicial power (reducing Viaux's sentence to two years, which was tantamount to declaring the collapse of legality in Chile), and of the comptroller's office (interpreting the law as requiring promulgation of the Congress-approved reform). All this had no counterpart in the government, which was more respectful of the laws than any in the last forty years, considering as it did that its chief source of strength lay in the legitimacy of its origin and the legality of its actions. In truth this proposition remained valid only as long as the division continued within the armed forces, for when the scales tipped decisively in favor of the "institutionalists," they needed no more pretexts to legitimize their action. On the other hand, the government's subordination to institutional machinery had a doubly disastrous result: demobilization of the popular organizations, and their impotence against the advancing military putschists. Far from becoming a tool at the service of the revolutionary process, the government became an end in itself—which explains the Communist Party's announcement in 1973, a few months before the final coup, of its concern about. . . the presidential elections of 1976.

By mid-1973 the institutional system was drained dry and Chile had to move on to new forms of organizing society. This was opportunely perceived by the more lucid reactionary elements represented by the employers' associations, as well as by revolutionary elements inside and outside of Popular Unity who were protesting and pushing for popular power. But while the former had the experience of decades of organizational, economic, political, and ideological predominance, plus their close relations with top military men, the latter had to start virtually from scratch and fight not only against the bourgeoisie but also against the institutionality that the government and Popular Unity leaders so ardently defended. Thus by September the reactionary theses loomed as a reality while the popular-power alternative was no more than a vigorous plant, growing but still very small and weak.

The dominant fraction in Popular Unity bears entire responsibility for the government's use of the institutional apparatus; and we can say that this policy achieved its maximum possibilities by causing bourgeois democracy to deepen and hence the popular movement to develop. But institutionality proved entirely inadequate to assure a revolutionary transformation of society, and ended as a potent obstacle to the working class and its struggle for socialism.

To sum up, we can describe the policy pursued as one of extreme strategic prudence which finally settled for indefinite postponement of the working class's historic objectives, including those partly envisaged in the Popular Unity government's basic program. It was a prudence dialectically complemented by extreme tactical adventurism in projecting goals which it had neither the necessary forces nor the indispensable alliances to implement. This line, blindly applied to the very end by the government and the top echelons of Popular Unity, led as if down a steep slope to the ideological and organizational disarming of workers dedicated to the revolutionary process.

Besides pointing out the basic respects in which the government's policy failed, it is also necessary to review the chief reasons for the profound antagonism of the bourgeoisie, for its decision to resort to destruction of its own institutions laboriously created and perfected throughout decades. We consider those reasons to have been the following: (1) the process of revolutionary organization and consciousness; (2)

the breach in the institutional structure; (3) the crisis of the economic system; (4) the global interest of imperialism; (5) the role assigned to the military.

Up to 1970 the organization of the Chilean working class and other working strata was a long and gradual process. From then on there was a steep rise in the number of unions, strikes, and occupations of land. But this movement was to a great extent controlled and directed by the government as a function of the tactic it pursued. Thus not only was it a secondary element auxiliary to the government's legal actions, but it was necessarily disciplined and responsible within the bounds of laws that continued in full force. It was the bourgeoisie itself that would give it a strong thrust and qualitatively modify the level of confrontation, by embarking on the insurrectional employer strike against the government in October 1972.

At that juncture forms of popular power arose that kept the society working despite the employer lockout and the dislocation of the state machine. The *cordones industriales, comandos comunales,* campesino councils, and other organic forms emerged as a real power which, while not managing to become an immediate alternative to state institutions, nevertheless began, with the post-June 1973 thrust, to pose a stronger challenge to the bourgeois model of domination than the government had ever achieved. In that period the organization and consciousness of Chilean workers, and of the urban proletariat in particular, reached the highest levels in Latin American history. They opened a road to a new democracy based not merely on numbers but also on the place occupied by the classes in society's productive process. These new structures had a superior potential for action, consciousness, formulating goals, and social reorganization.

For the bourgeoisie, popular power was a danger, an intolerable threat. It was precisely the democracy existing in Chile and strengthened during the Allende government that had enabled this power to emerge and that manifestly could not halt it. And when the representatives of the bourgeoisie attacked "parallel armies" and, insistently appealed to the armed forces, their object was precisely to break the popular-power nuclei which were the biggest potential threat to their system of domination.

To cut off the development of popular power, the bourgeoisie had to do away with democracy. And since the government would not play this role, it too had to be done away with to make room for one that would.

The rupture of harmonious institutionality in Chile was extremely dangerous for the bourgeoisie as a whole. Traditionally, that institutionality had been on the one hand the regulator of the different owning strata's varying interests, and on the other the instrument to hold the workers down. With the capture of executive power by the workers' parties, those two indispensable values had been lost to the ruling class, which was prepared to yield the state apparatus to reformists, whether bourgeois or worker, provided that they administered capitalist society efficiently. But the thrust and dynamic of the popular movement, plus the presence of the revolutionary current, reinforced the transformational content of Popular Unity's program. In that situation the bourgeoisie used the institutionality it controlled to oppose the government's management of the state, and the rupture of institutionality was brought about well before the National and Christian Democratic parties provoked the armed forces to stop constitutional realization of Allende's program by seizing power. This brought into the open the real content of capitalist state institutions and the limitations of democracy, which became effective barriers to a new organization of society. After October 1972 Chilean institutionality betrayed its exhaustion and it became the bourgeoisie's urgent task to find new forms for maintenance of its power. In the end, facing as it did the breakdown of its studiously perfected constitutional regulator, the only answer it found was the arbitrary power of military force.

The system by which it had maintained a delicate "democratic" equilibrium for forty years proved absolutely ineffectual to bring about a new equilibrium not based on bourgeois hegemony. And since the old institutionality could not cope with the challenge to the bourgeois model of domination, it was now indispensable for the bourgeoisie to regain absolute control of the state apparatus, to reorient society for the new and pressing tasks which in that class's interest could admit of no delay.

The economic crisis was no secondary reason for the rupture of the constitutional system. Beginning in mid-1972 the bourgeoisie dedicated itself with renewed élan to the demolition of normality to stop the government from strengthening its redistribution model, and won to its cause broad petty-bourgeois proprietor sectors and almost all middle entrepreneurs. From that time on, the relations of production and trade were characterized by the total absence of productive investments and the channeling of all profits and some capital into hoarding and speculation. But this was plainly a transitory situation that would give way at a given moment to renewed accumulation and development of the means of production.

Furthermore, the modernizing tendencies of world capitalism required a new model in which state participation was a primary element in the economy, integrated with and at the service of the long-term interests of multinational enterprises as well as of the native monopolist bourgeoisie. Consequently, the employer organizations needed state institutions not only to guarantee their property, but as the sole means of regulating internal contradictions and reordering Chile's production and trade structure in line with the new capitalist characteristics emerging in Latin America—the increasingly strong tendencies to a state role in production and new relationships between countries of the "periphery."

In point of fact, the "developmental" models postulating agreements on terms of trade and a complementary relationship between "national bourgeoisies" and the multinationals were obsolete, unviable, unreal schemes in the dynamic of the present period. The multinationals' growing activity was part of a new stage of world capitalism characterized by extreme internationalization of the economy and by integration at all levels. In this new situation the multinationals became economic "universes" with budgets far above the Chilean state's, with voluminous and fluid "internal" relations between their diverse components and technology transfers aimed at opening and exploiting new markets, integrating and planning them as a function of their autonomous interests which embraced the most varied and complex fields.

This superinternationalist phase of capitalism, the result of the extraordinary advance of productive forces, was precisely aimed at avoiding periodic crises and recessions and halting the decline of the rate of profit which so often brings them on.

The multinationals' impact on the Latin American countries' weak productive, financial, and commercial structures further intensified their subordination and their dependency on external factors—technology, machinery and replacements, capital, fiscal and trade policies, market, lifestyles. It speeded up even more the concentration of income within a small sector and further reduced the consumer potential of most of the population.

These tendencies, added to the huge growth of the foreign debt in the last Frei period, aggravated Chile's social and political tensions to the maximum. Consequently, the break that was initiated with U.S. imperialism and the multinationals also imperiled the survival of the bourgeoisie. The Chilean bourgeois class realized it could not resist the blockade that was to be expected as a result of the popular government's policy and the response already evoked from the big copper concerns. And it was only possible to extend this model of highly subordinated integration into the world capitalist economic system, and obtain new sources of accumulation for division between multinationals and the top Chilean entrepreneurs, by superexploitation of the workers and their total political subjection as an imperative precondition.

U.S. imperialism was not solely concerned to defend its interests in Chile; equally or more important was the "equilibrium" of the whole South American strategic region, threatened by the revolutionary process. The attempt to change Chile's socioeconomic structures by the method we have studied was in fact the final expression—and the most profound, serious, and perfected one—of a whole period of great tensions and instabilities in Latin America. Hence Popular Unity's victory brought danger to the doorstep of all Southern Cone regimes, whose people saw as a beacon of hope the new possibilities for an epoch of independence, democracy, and justice. The initial perspective of the socialism-building process greatly strengthened revolutionary tendencies among workers of neighboring states: Peru, Bolivia, and especially Argentina, countries where the surge of popular struggles had simultaneously weakened bourgeois domination.

The U.S. government and its counter-revolutionary organizations, the CIA and Naval Intelligence, acted to "destabilize" the Chilean government and bring it down. And we have noted the similar efforts in the economic field of private and public U.S. organizations, which in addition had big interests to defend, such as the multinationals ITT, Kennecott, and Anaconda. The popular government acted with extreme prudence in international relations, and while it maintained "good relations" with neighbor governments, it is equally true that the whole area was marked at this time by great instability which only the armed forces of the countries in question could control.

By whatever means, the U.S. government had to stop Allende's government from securing itself, or face a situation in its southern "backyard" which, for all its specific features, would have shared some general characteristics with the then-current crisis in Southeast Asia.

The aims and interests of U.S. imperialist strategy, as partially defined for Latin America in the Rockefeller Report, go far to explain its relations with Chile, the mechanics of which have come to public knowledge in revelations about the activities of global counter-revolutionary services under U.S. direction.

For forty years Chile's bourgeoisie was sincerely "civic-minded," even relegating the military to a second-string role of low prestige in Chilean society. Management of state affairs was indeed in safe hands while liberal, radical, populist, conservative, and Christian Democratic governments succeeded one another, and the good offices of the armed institutions were not needed. But from the very day of Salvador Allende's election, the military moved into an unanticipated stellar role, and the state repressive apparatus once more became the last bastion of the Chilean bourgeoisie's values and the arbiter of the nation's destinies.

By force of circumstance—or, more precisely, as a result of its political tactic—the popular government only reinforced the participation of top officers in government decisions: it brought them into the cabinet in November 1972 and from that moment reactionaries and reformists always sought to heighten the military influence. The new role they undertook acquired its own dynamic, and all ranks in the armed forces, having first set themselves up as arbiters, soon felt called upon to run the country. Thus the constitutional precepts of obedience and discipline went by the board on all levels, and general discussion raged in which the reactionary tendency was stimulated among officers of the three services and the resistance to it among NCOs and other ranks was strangled at birth.

The role assigned to the top officers generated its own force, and their ambitions put an end not only to the constitutional regime but also—at least for a time—to the intermediary role of right-wing politicians and bureaucrats who to all appearances had a firm and stable place in the state superstructure.

The government's failure and the causes of the coup d'état do not suffice to explain the interruption and defeat of the revolutionary process; this also had its own dynamic which, with all its strengths and weaknesses due to other mentioned factors, to a certain extent ran on its own rails. We believe that Chile's history during the Popular Unity government offers three basic reasons for the workers' failure to affirm their predominance in the society and to begin building socialism: (1)

the weakness of the political revolutionary vanguard; (2) the meager development of an alternative power to bourgeois institutionality; (3) the unity of the repressive apparatus dependent on the capitalist state.

To conduct their struggles, the working class and the workers need ideological education, leadership for their day-to-day demands, goals that are not lost to sight in fighting a thousand small battles, an organization enabling confrontations to be coordinated on a national scale by unifying in time and space efforts that otherwise, in isolation, become diluted and lose energy and content. In other words, in the struggle for socialism the workers need a general staff to educate, discipline, organize, and lead the confrontation in specific situations—a revolutionary vanguard to defend their historic goals and strategic objectives, and to assure the irreversibility of proletarian gains on all levels.

Potentially, the Chilean revolutionary vanguard consisted of those who did not go along with—and hence were not responsible for the failure of—the policy followed by the government and the top echelons of Popular Unity, that is, MAPU, Christian Left, a sector of the Socialist Party, and MIR. However, these organizations—or tendencies within them, as in the case of the Socialist Left during the whole period and of MAPU up to March 1973—did not succeed in coordinating their actions, establishing common tactical objectives, or even proposing unification of their forces. Consequently, they never managed to set up a true leadership but limited themselves to challenging the policies of the government alliance. Furthermore, only on rare occasions did that challenge take an open critical form, and this helped to keep the masses in a state of ambiguity which was also characteristic of the Left and prevented it from overcoming the influence of the Popular Unity leadership's line. The education, discipline, and organization promoted by Chile's revolutionary forces were quite inadequate for the magnitude of the tasks they were set, and the coherence and firmness of their positions were also weakened by the lack of a firm decision to present an alternative model to the masses. The illusion and the rhetorical use of unity slogans—actually unity around the positions of the Communist Party—kept the revolutionary organizations, especially the Socialist Left, from energetically putting forward their own positions and building unity around revolution. Thus the weakness of the vanguard prevented it from forging an organization out of the Chilean workers' countless expressions of courage, vigor, enthusiasm, and consciousness, and became the chief factor in the frustration of the revolutionary process.

We have noted the different forms of popular power that the Chilean workers built during the popular government period, forms which developed and grew precisely in situations of sharpest confrontation with the bourgeoisie. Popular power really existed in Chile and was clearly expressed as the capacity to act upon society outside of state mechanisms consecrated by the Constitution.

However, this popular power was not perfected enough to become an overall alternative power to bourgeois institutionality. There were two basic reasons for this. First was the resistance to it, the brake imposed on it by a government-Popular Unity sector who feared to see their tactical plan superseded by a dynamic they did not control. The hold that this sector had over a part of the workers took forces away from the development of popular power, and when it decided to promote popular power together with the revolutionary Left against the reactionary onslaught at the end of June, it was already too late to structure any centralized national organism which would present to the whole country its own model of development and power. A government charged with illegitimacy by the institutional bourgeoisie confronted that institutionality, and no power existed that could achieve nationwide organization of the society on a contrary course. Thus the revolutionary process lacked the indispensable instrument to lead the country and subdue the resistance of the exploiting classes. The existence of popular power was only a potential threat to the prevailing order, never becoming an immediate and effective alternative—a situation in which the weakness of the revolutionary vanguard certainly played no small part.

The unity of the repressive state apparatus at the service of counter-revolution was definitely the result of the government's military policy. The split between "constitutionalists" and "institutionalists" was shown to be a basic element of the tactic pursued; so that when the tactic was defeated by the bourgeois institutionality that surrounded it on all fronts, the line with respect to the armed forces was likewise defeated.

Only late in the day—because of the submission to the myths of "professionalism" and the military's "obedience to the government"—was an attempt made to bring revolutionary positions to the NCOs, enlisted men, and officers for discussion; thus reaction and reformism had a free field to spread their ideology in military establishments. When there was an effort to promote revolutionary resistance to the putschists, retreat had already begun and the putschists had a free hand in brutally nipping it in the bud.

Once again, the concessions and weaknesses of Chile's revolutionary political organizations ended by confirming that a process of deep changes, and the capture of power for a qualitative change in society, are possible only if the repressive apparatus is split and one part of it won over by the workers' courage, political consciousness, fighting determination, and material organization.

With all its special peculiarities, the Chilean experience shows the full validity of a theory repeatedly confirmed, set forth by one of the founders of the revolutionary socialist movement, Frederick Engels:

> According to the philosophical notion, the state is the "realisation of the idea" or the Kingdom of God on earth, translated into philosophical terms, the sphere in which eternal truth and justice is or should be realised. And from this follows a superstitious reverence for the state and everything connected with it, which takes root the more readily as people from their childhood are accustomed to imagine that the affairs and interests common to the whole of society could not be looked after otherwise than as they have been looked after in the past, that is, through the state and its well-paid officials. And people think they have taken quite an extraordinarily bold step forward when they have rid themselves of belief in hereditary monarchy and swear by the democratic republic. In reality, however, the state is nothing but a machine for the oppression of one class by another, and indeed in the democratic republic no less than in the monarchy; and at best an evil inherited by the proletariat after its victorious struggle for class supremacy, whose worst sides the proletariat, just like the Commune, cannot avoid having to lop off at the earliest possible moment, until such time as a new generation, reared in new and free social conditions, will be able to throw the entire lumber of the state on the scrap-heap.[1]

1. Frederick Engels, introduction to Karl Marx, *The Civil War in France* (New York: International Publishers, 1940).